GOD IN IMAX:
A PANORAMA OF DIVINE HISTORY

R O N   S A N D E R S

Ron Sanders
Psalm 19:1-2
6/4/2015

PAGE PUBLISHING, INC.
New York, NY

First originally published by Page Publishing, Inc. 2015

ISBN 978-1-63417-745-0 (pbk)
ISBN 978-1-63417-746-7 (digital)

Printed in the United States of America

CONTENTS

ACKNOWLEDGMENTS

When one writes much depends on the impact others have made on your life. First I would like to acknowledge my wife. During her life she has given herself to the care of many. This book is dedicated to her for her service and help to the author and many others.

Most engineers are not noted for their writing skills. I owe much for the help of Ellen Bartelli, a friend and High School English teacher. Ellen shared many writing tips, and also proof read the manuscript.

Lastly I appreciate those who endorsed my work. My wife and I worked under the direction of Jean Nystrand retired Executive Director of BSF International. Jean stressed individual study of the scriptures, and application of Biblical principles to one's daily life. Sitting under the teaching of Dr. Toussaint caused me to see the Bible as a word direct from God, and worthy of a lifetime of study. We have partnered with Garth Gustafson in his work in Cambodia. Garth is proving that there is power in a knowledge of scripture to change lives for the better, in a land where there has been little knowledge of the Bible in the past. I became acquainted with Colonel Jacobs while we worked together in the Air Force. He has been an inspiration to us and a lifetime friendship has resulted. Retiring from the Air Force he has become more involved in the spiritual war, recently departing for the mission field.

PREFACE

My wife grew up with three brothers and says, "It is better to be abused than to be ignored." She also says, "Those who love you are the biggest teases." It seems this becomes truer when your hair begins to turn colors. Age often becomes a catalyst for others to taunt a person. I have been accused of "being older than dirt." Now, that is very close to "In the beginning." The same person, when preparing for a class in Genesis, called my wife to say, "I am studying creation, and I need some answers from an eye witness." No, in spite of the gray hair, we can't be pushed back to Genesis; however, we, like all those who know Jesus Christ as Savior, do know and have access to one who was an eye witness to creation. At the beginning of all things, we are introduced to God Himself. "In the beginning GOD…"

THE AUTHOR OF CREATION   CHAP. 1

To understand what is happening around us, it is necessary to know something about the One, who planned it all and is carrying history to its climax. Furthermore, we can only know what God is like by what He has revealed to us about Himself. We can understand certain things about God since He created us in His own image and likeness. In many ways, God has made us similar to Himself, which assures us that it is possible for people to have a relationship with God; however, there are characteristics about God that are far beyond our understanding. These attributes of God may be defined as characteristics of God's divine nature and are true of no other being. In order to better understand God, I will divide His attributes into two classifications: incommunicable and communicable.

First, there are characteristics of God that are true only of Him and that He has not shared with anyone else. God is a spirit, without physical form (John 4:24). He cannot be limited. God is self-existent, independent of everything else, and does not depend on anyone or anything for His being. Because of His independence of being, He causes everything to depend on Him. In a universe of change, only God is immutable. Since He is perfect, God is also devoid of all change. This truth is of enormous importance. Since God never changes, His love and promises to His people are forever certain.

Being eternal, God is not limited to temporal limitations. Psalm 90:2 expressed this: "Before the mountains were brought forth, or ever you had formed the earth and the world, from everlasting to everlasting you are God."

God said to Moses, "I am who I am." And he said, "Say this to the people of Israel, 'I am has sent me to you.'" (Exod. 3:14 English Standard Version)

What God is telling Moses—and conversely to us—is that He has always existed. As God is not limited to time, neither is He limited to space. The doctrine of omnipresence tells us God is in all places, being everywhere. Psalm 139:7–9 states: "Where can I go from Your Spirit? Where can I flee from Your presence? If I go up to the heavens, You are there; if I make my bed in the depths, You are there." God's presence penetrates and fills the entire universe. This is also true of the earth and should comfort the believer, knowing that no calamity can happen to him without God being present with him.

Unlike us, God doesn't forget or come up short on understanding. The English word for this characteristic is omniscience (omni meaning "all" and science meaning "knowledge"). God has all knowledge—or maybe better said—God knows all things. This is not limited to the present but stretches from the beginning of time to eternity.

> O Lord, you have searched me and known me! You know when I sit down and when I rise up; you discern my thoughts from afar. You search out my path and my lying down and are acquainted with all my ways. Even before a word is on my tongue, behold, O Lord, you know it altogether. (Ps. 139:1–4)

And the third "omni" is omnipotence. God is all-powerful and able to do whatever He wills. God is said to be almighty, which relates to His omnipotence. He who created the heavens can do all things; nothing is too hard for Him.

Ah, Lord God! It is you who have made the heavens and the earth by your great power and by your outstretched arm! Nothing is too hard for you. (Jer. 32:17)

The extent of the universe has never been determined despite scientific discoveries and the launching of the Hubble Space Telescope and the Voyager 1 and 2. The fact is that new discoveries only show that the universe is still larger than earlier thought. A question that has confronted man is, Why isn't there just nothing? Without question, the universe and all that it contains definitely exists. The law of cause and effect states: "Every natural event has a natural cause." This leaves us with the question: what could have caused our universe, which is of such great magnitude? The second rule of the law of cause and effect is that "no effect can be greater than its cause." Knowing that the universe is of great size and that its motions are well orchestrated, we can only conclude that the universe's cause is beyond our imagination.

We can search far and wide for the cause of the universe, but the only reasonable answer is the answer provided by the Bible. The God, who is eternal (and therefore not limited to time), is all-knowing and all-present; and the God, who has unlimited power, is the one who caused or created the universe and all things in it. Only He is greater than all the created things that surround us. The God of the Bible is not only a God of creation; he is a God of relations. He is not a transcendent or distant God who does not care. He is near and desires a relationship with us.

> You hem me in, behind and before, and lay your
> hand upon me. Such knowledge is too wonderful
> for me; it is high; I cannot attain it. Where shall
> I go from your Spirit? Or where shall I flee from
> your presence? (Ps. 139:5–7)

Being a God who desires a relationship with His creatures, He is seen far differently than the gods of other cultures and religions. The concepts of god are numerous from monotheism, pantheism, polytheism, deism, atheism, etc. The Bible pictures a triune God. This is a strange concept to many. I have even been told, "It is ridiculous to worship a three-headed god." But if a person knows the characteristics of God, it could be no other way. Our God is said to be self-sufficient and also a God of love. If God is self-sufficient, He has need of nothing and is complete in Himself. Being a God of love, our God needs an object upon which He can express His love. If He does not have this object, then He is not self-sufficient. Logic requires a pluralistic God; the Bible tells of a triune God. He is a God who consists of one essence manifested in three persons: Father, Son, and Holy Spirit. A God, who is completely self-sufficient, with the three divine persons loving each other from eternity past.

Being a loving God, God has created other personal beings with whom He could have a relationship. In order to accomplish this, He created mankind in His own image and likeness (Genesis 1:26). By creating personal beings in His own image, God shares many of His characteristics and attributes with these beings thus making relationships possible; thus, we have a second category of attributes, which have been communicated to us not in the full extent that these attributes are true of God but to a lesser degree in those God has created.

Some of the communicable attributes are love, knowledge, wisdom, goodness, holiness, mercy, truth, and righteousness. God loves unconditionally but has given us a capacity to love, to display goodness, and to show mercy. He is all-knowing; but we can learn, attain knowledge, and exhibit wisdom. God is absolutely holy and righteous, but having given believers new birth, he commands us to be likewise. God is the author of truth. From the days of Pilate (John 18:38) until today, absolutes are denied; however, truth is truth regardless of the numbers who deny there is truth. God's character demands no deviation from truth thus requiring absolutes. This gives us a small glimpse of the author of creation.

THE FIRST ORDER OF PERSONAL CREATION   CHAP. 2

During the past century, two issues stood out among those that have been debated by scientists and theologians: (1) Is there life in the universe outside of the earth? (2) What is the age of the earth? It seems that on these issues both sides have a degree of truth and might learn from each other, except for their stubborn resistance and unwillingness to accept the facts that show they might have a lack of knowledge themselves. Although the Bible speaks mainly about God's relationship with people, there are often blips of truth in scattered verses that will give us an answer to these questions. Regarding the first question Is there life in the universe outside of the earth?, the Bible says a definite yes. Is there physical human life beyond the earth? No. We will deal with this issue more fully in chapter 3.

The Bible speaks often of spiritual personal beings that are known as angels. We can get an idea of some of the activity of angels in the first two chapters of Job.

> Now there was a day when the sons of God came to present themselves before the Lord, and Satan also came among them. The Lord said to Satan, "From where have you come?" Satan answered the Lord

and said, "From going to and fro on the earth, and
from walking up and down on it" (Job 1:6–7)

Again there was a day when the sons of God came
to present themselves before the Lord, and Satan
also came among them to present himself before
the Lord. And the Lord said to Satan, "From where
have you come?" Satan answered the Lord and said,
"From going to and fro on the earth, and from
walking up and down on it." (Job 2:1–2)

To understand what is happening here, we must answer two questions: who are the "sons of God," and why are they coming before
God? In the New Testament, the term "sons of God" is used for believers; however, this is not true in the Old Testament. We do know they
were joined with Satan as they came before God. We do know Satan
is an angelic being, thus the preferred view that the "sons of God" are
angels. Satan tells God he has been roaming about the earth. Satan is
also known as the god of this world.

And even if our gospel is veiled, it is veiled to those
who are perishing. In their case the god of this
world has blinded the minds of the unbelievers, to
keep them from seeing the light of the gospel of the
glory of Christ, who is the image of God. (2 Cor.
4:3–4)

It seems that the earth was Satan's realm, and he was reporting to
God what was happening there. With this being the case, we can assure
the other angels were reporting the activities in their realms throughout
the universe. Yes, there is life beyond the earth; but it is angelic life, and
these angels are busy superintending God's universe.

What is the age of the earth? Again, a verse in Job gives us some
insight.

Then the Lord answered Job out of the whirlwind
and said: "Who is this that darkens counsel by words
without knowledge? Dress for action like a man;

and I will question you, and you make it known to me. Where were you when I laid the foundation of the earth? Tell me, if you have understanding. Who determined its measurements—surely you know!

Or who stretched the line upon it? On what were its bases sunk, or who laid its cornerstone, when the morning stars sang together and all the sons of God shouted for joy?..." (Job 38:1–7)

God is rebuking Job in these verses for being overly self-confident. He questions Job about his knowledge of the foundations of the earth upon which Job was sitting. God goes on to say when the earth's foundations were laid, the "morning stars" and "sons of God" were already there, singing and shouting for joy. We already know that the "sons of God" are angels. In scripture, there is a connection between stars and heavenly bodies and angels; so it is assumed that the "morning stars are also angels.

Praise the Lord! Praise the Lord from the heavens; praise him in the heights! Praise him, all his *angels*; praise him, all his hosts! Praise him, sun and moon; praise him, all you shining *stars*! (Psalm 148:1–3)

The angels were there when God was establishing the foundation of the earth upon which Job was sitting—The same earth we today stand upon and the same earth Adam and Eve stood upon. This being the case, angels had to be created before man. And the universe that they superintended for God was created before the earth was reformed to what we have known it to be.

What did the universe that the angels superintended for God look like? Really, we have no way of knowing exactly; however, with the era of the Hubble Space Telescope and Voyager 1 and 2, we now have pictures of portions of the universe. From these pictures, it seems safe to assume that the universe has always been quite similar. In the pictures available, we see magnificent spectrums of color caused by light radiating from these solar bodies and galaxies. These bodies, science tells us, are made up of various gases, dust, ice, and solid rock materials composed of the many chemicals we learned about in our chemistry classes. The earth that we have said was Satan's realm, at that time, was not the beautiful blue planet we know today. Very likely at that time, it compared to the other solar bodies. Think of it being a huge rock covered by an ocean of ice. It too was a beautiful site at that time—as light radiated off the ice, causing a beautiful spectrum of colors.

Is there any evidence that an ocean of ice covered the early earth? Today as scientists search for life in the universe, they look for water, which is necessary for life as we know it. The problem is not water in the universe but liquid water. Water is found throughout the universe, but the problem is that it is solid ice. Examples of this ice are the rings of Saturn and the moons of several of the planets in our own solar system.

The Bible does not focus on angels. The Bible is written for men and women for the purpose of leading us into a relationship with God. Angels are often spoken of in the Bible but, primarily, regarding how they affect man. Scriptures do give us glimpses of the actions of angels in their early relationship with God, but to understand these early relationships between God and angels, there is a need to look at God's character and his reason for creating personal beings. We know God created man in His own image and likeness in order to have a relationship with him. It seems safe to assume that God created angels, who are also created personal beings, for the same reason. This is also borne out by the fact that the angels were reporting their activities to God in the first two chapters of Job.

How long this harmonious relationship between God and angels continued, we have no way of knowing since the scriptures are silent on this point. We do know God is eternal; therefore, it is not unreasonable to assume this relationship continued for a long time. We do know that harmony was disrupted by sin and disobedience in the angelic ranks. It began with Lucifer, who sought to take over God's place.

> "How you are fallen from heaven, O Lucifer Day Star, son of Dawn! How you are cut down to the ground, you who laid the nations low! You said in your heart: 'I will ascend to heaven; above the

stars of God I will set my throne on high; I will sit on the mount of assembly in the far reaches of the north; I will ascend above the heights of the clouds; I will make myself like the Most High.' But you are brought down to Sheol, to the far reaches of the pit...." (Isa. 14:12–15)

With Lucifer's disobedience, sin spread though the angelic realms until it had involved one-third of the angelic ranks.

And another sign appeared in heaven: behold, a great red dragon, with seven heads and ten horns, and on his heads seven diadems. His tail swept down a third of the stars of heaven and cast them to the earth.... (Rev. 12: 3–4)

This angelic person, Lucifer, needs to be explained. Who is he? He is the one who, with his disobedience, became Satan. From being known as The Bright and Shiny One, Satan became the dastardly "Master of Darkness." The prophet Ezekiel gives us some information of Lucifer's original position and status.

"You were the signet of perfection, full of wisdom and perfect in beauty. You were in Eden, the garden of God; every precious stone was your covering, sardius, topaz, and diamond beryl, onyx, and jasper, sapphire, emerald, and carbuncle; and crafted in gold were your settings and your engravings. On the day that you were created they were prepared. You were an anointed guardian cherub. I placed you; you were on the holy mountain of God; in the midst of the stones of fire you walked. You were blameless in your ways from the day you were created, till unrighteousness was found in you. In the abundance of your trade you were filled with violence in your midst, and you sinned; I cast you as a profane thing from the mountain of God, and I destroyed you, O guardian cherub, from the midst of the stones of fire. Your heart was proud because of your beauty; you corrupted your wisdom for the sake of your splendor. I cast you to the ground; I expose you before kings, to feast their eyes on you...." (Ezek. 28:12–17)

Originally Satan was a perfect creature. He was in Eden (there as a tempter). Being the anointed cherub who covers seems to speak of him having a position before God and God's throne. To get an understanding of this, we need to look at the Ark of the Covenant, which was placed in the Holy of Holies in the tabernacle. The construction of the ark is explained in Exodus.

Bezalel made the ark of acacia wood. Two cubits and a half was its length, a cubit and a half its breadth, and a cubit and a half its height. And he overlaid it with pure gold inside and outside, and made a molding of gold around it. And he cast for it four rings of gold for its four feet, two rings on its one side and two rings on its other side. He made poles of acacia wood and overlaid them with gold and put the poles into the rings on the sides of the ark to carry the ark. And he made a mercy seat of pure gold. Two cubits and a half was its length, and a cubit and a half its breadth. And he made two cherubim of gold. He made them of hammered work at the two ends of the mercy seat, one cherub on the one end, and one cherub on the other end. Of one piece with the mercy seat he made the cherubim at its two ends. The cherubim spread out their wings above, overshadowing the mercy seat with their wings, with their faces one to another; toward the mercy seat were the faces of the cherubim. (Exod. 37:1–9)

The Ark of the Covenant represented the presence of God, and over the Ark hovered two cherubim, which symbolized angels protecting the holiness of God. Think of the changing of the guard at Buckingham Palace. Really, those two guards offer little protection to the Queen. Their position is an honorary one. Our omnipotent God does not need any protection, so really, Lucifer's position as the covering cherub seems to be a position of honor. Being near God must have not been enough for this one, caught up in the beauty Ezekiel describes of Lucifer. Dissatisfied, he sets out to replace God (as stated in the aforementioned verse from Isaiah).

Let's also consider another possible cause of Lucifer's demise, which resulted from his pride. We already know that Satan is also called the god of this world (2 Cor. 4:4). Comparing Earth with the other planets in our solar system, it is medium-sized, but compared to our sun it is quite small. The sun has a diameter 109 times the size of the earth. The sun seems very large; but looking out into the universe, we find stars like Pollux, Arcturus, Rigel, Aldebaran, Beetlejuice, and Antares—all of which dwarf our sun. Antares has a radius approximately 883 times the size of our sun and is roughly 550 light-years away from the earth. If Antares was placed in the center of our solar system, its outer edge would lie somewhere between the orbits of Mars and Jupiter. When Earth is placed on a scale with these solar bodies, it becomes a speck so small that it cannot be seen. Did you ever wonder if Satan compared the size of his realm with that of the other angels? Can you hear him saying "God, look at how capable I am, and you give me that speck, the earth, to superintend? God, you are not fair"? One thing we can be certain of is that he thought he could do a better job than God, so he set out to be "like the Most High."

With Satan's rebellion, a spiritual warfare, which continues to this day, began. There is a lesson here of which we need to take notice. To take sides against God will never bring about good. Satan's rebellion has only brought destruction, hurt, pain, death, and everything that is harmful. We have a choice to follow God and enjoy His goodness or to proceed on a wayward course; only do not expect any results different from those caused by Satan's rebellion.

THE SECOND ORDER OF PERSONAL CREATION

CHAP. 3

Disobedience causes trouble, and Satan's turning from God was a disaster that has raged throughout the ages and continues unabated in our day. Spiritual war dominates all areas of life today. The following question is asked: why didn't God deal with Satan? Answer: He will. When: Only He knows. Why wait? Because God has a better plan, which we will begin to look into.

Spiritual warfare is concentrated on the earth, which is Satan's realm, but scripture seems to indicate that it extends into the universe. To lead His attack on sin, evil, and disobedience, God created a new order of personal being who was to gain dominion, Man.

> Then God said, "Let us make man in our image, after our likeness. And let them have *dominion* over the fish of the sea and over the birds of the heavens and over the livestock and *over all the earth* and over every creeping thing that creeps on the earth." So God created man in his own image, in the image of God he created him; male and female he created them. And God blessed them. And God

said to them, "Be fruitful and multiply and fill the earth and *subdue it*, and have *dominion* over the fish of the sea and over the birds of the heavens and over every living thing that moves on the earth." (Gen. 1:26–28)

God's first order of personal life was spiritual beings—angels. God's new order of living beings would be physical-spiritual beings— men and women. We will look at His reason for this later in this chapter. Man being a physical being required a new environment, which had not previously existed, in order to live. Before creating man, God set out to establish such an environment. This He did in the six days of creation that is explained in Genesis 1. Since the sin problem began with Lucifer (Satan), whose realm was the earth, God refurbished the earth to support physical life. The reason for this would be that on the earth, God would work out His plan to overcome sin and rebellion.

A great deal of debate surrounds this work of God. Did God even create this earth, or did everything just evolve? How old is the earth? We have both "old Earth" and "young Earth" theorists. Did the earth come about in six literal days, or did each segment of the earth's development take long eras?

In the first area of debate, we need to affirm the universe exists and why there is not nothing or a vast void. Everyone will affirm the universe exists. Two possibilities exist: (1) someone made it, or (2) the material in the universe has eternally existed. Today the most accepted theory for the existence of the universe is the Big Bang, which clearly states that the universe had a beginning and will have an ending. It is well accepted that the material universe is not eternal. The only alternative is that the universe had a cause. The second rule of the law of cause and effect is "the cause must be greater than the effect." No one questions the great magnitude of the universe. We must ask, "Are the slow progresses which are attributed to evolution greater than the universe and all its creatures?" It takes a great imagination to even begin to think so. When we look at the age of our earth and the magnitude of the universe, the answers given in scripture for the cause and beginning of the universe seem much more reasonable to explain all that we see. Only a wise and omnipotent God could make what we see happen.

Concerning the age of the earth it seems that both the old and young Earthers are locked into their narrow frames of references and refuse to consider all the evidence. Those who hold to an old Earth basically hold to the theories of evolution, which are built on a foundation of uniformitarianism. The basic premise of uniformitarianism is that the processes that we see happening on the earth today have been the same throughout the long ages of the past. Evolutionists surmise that given enough time anything can happen. Experience, however, does not bear this out. Time brings decay, not renewal. Time brings death, not life.

Those who hold to the great age of the earth base their thinking on the rock structure over the earth and the fossils contained therein. These same people discount the Bible as having any authority. They say Bible believers argue in a circle saying, "The Bible is the word of God because the Bible says it is the world of God." These critics of the Bible do the same, arguing in a circle. They say that rocks across the earth are old because the fossils in them are old, and the fossils are old because the rocks that contain them are old.

I would like to share my experience growing up in the midland prairies of the USA. I was raised in Nebraska, exactly 100 years after the Oregon Trail was being established. At that time, the trail had reached Fort Hall in Idaho and was being pushed on to Oregon. History books are replete with stories of the great herds of buffalo that roamed the exact area where I grew up. My grandfather told stories of his boyhood when men he knew told of these great herds. A popular song of my boyhood was "Home on the Range." I loved the lyrics below:

> Oh, give me a home where the buffalo roam,
> Where the deer and the antelope play,
> Where seldom is heard a discouraging word
> And the sky is not cloudy all day.

Although this song was very applicable to Nebraska and the area where I lived, to my surprise, I have found it is the state song of Kansas. This only proves that these herds of buffalo were far more numerous than even I expected. The real surprise, though, was in my early days; I found no evidence that buffalos ever existed. No evidence at all—not a hide, not a bone, not even a fossil! To add weight to this matter, others of my time were baffled by lack of evidence for the existence of buffalos across the midlands of the USA. I was beginning to think that the buffalo might have been some mythical creature similar to the Loch Ness Monster; then one summer, our family took a vacation to visit an aunt living in the Black Hills of South Dakota. We were driving through the *Wind Cave National Park* and all of a sudden, there they were. Buffalos were real—saved from extinction in this national reserve for their preservation.

So is there any significance to my story? I was left with a question: if four to five hundred years of uniform conditions in the midlands had not resulted in one buffalo fossil, would one to two billion years of uniform conditions result in the many fossils we find in our world today? The answer I came to was a resounding no. For fossils to form, there is need for creatures to be suddenly buried; and uniform conditions do not provide that mechanism. The following question could be asked: how then do you explain the fact that fossils are found around the world? That question will be answered in chapter 6. The earth has been around for a long time, but the fossils are not an indication of its age. It was created when God made a realm for his angels. How old, we do not know; but God is eternal, which suggests it could be very old.

The young Earth theorists say everything we see in the universe began with the six days of creation (Genesis 1). I agree that the earth as we see it today became that way as described in Genesis 1; however, shouldn't we allow that the God, who is almighty, might have had something going before He created physical human life of which we are a part? We will say more about this in chapter 4. The youth Earthers expound that to say that the earth has great age is only to accommodate evolution. With some, who hold to an old Earth, this may be true; but I think we have shown that the earth can have long age apart from any thoughts of evolution.

Now to deal with the third question; was the length of a day, as used in Genesis 1, a 24-hour day or long eras? It is true that the Bible used the term "day" both ways. Today we also do the same. We think of a day as a 24-hour period of time. We also speak of "The Day of George Washington," the period of time when George Washington was living.

It is interesting that the Bible also uses the term day in this way when referring to time. A week is always seven days; a month, 30 days; and a year, 360 days (on the Jewish calendar). But day is used both ways. The issue of the length of a day in Genesis is not even debatable unless one caves in to the theistic evolutionist, who demands greater time as he tries to make the Bible and evolution compatible. A period of time marked out as "evening and morning" and called day has always been a 24-hour period of time.

In creating man to lead the battle of spiritual warfare, God also created a personal being to whom He could relate. Being created in the image of God, man was given many characteristics that were also true of God so that man would be able to relate to God; however in one way, man is unique, and he was differed from God and the angels who were before him. Man was a physical being.

Why did God make man different? Let's study God's purpose and plan. God is looking for a relationship with His creatures. He does not want robots or puppets that will do whatever He wants when He pulls the strings. God gave angels and man free will so they would relate to Him willingly. Free will makes it possible to rebel, which was the case with Lucifer and the disobedient angels who followed him. God knew that by giving man free will, man could also disobey. Knowing this, God made man different—a physical being.

Let's look at God's wisdom in doing this. With angels, who are spiritual beings, there seems to be no redemption for rebellion. Lucifer and the angels who followed him sinned in innocent perfection. They had been in the presence of God and still struck out against Him. Angels have no end, and it seems once they have rebelled, their rebellion or their attitudes do not change. The Bible speaks of no redemption for them. God has even prepared for angel's separation from Himself. This is shown in the following verse from Matthew 25:41:

> "Then He [Jesus] will say to those on *his* left, 'Depart from me, you cursed, into the eternal fire prepared for the *devil and his angels*....'"

Look at Satan; even when he knows his time is short (as stated in Revelation 12:12), he continues his rebellious and destructive ways. It seems he will be cast into the "Lake of Fire," kicking and screaming.

God knew that if man had free will, he could choose to be disobedient and prolong the sin problem. Knowing this, God had a foolproof backup plan. To accomplish this plan, God made man a physical being. Should man sin, there would be a price to pay.

> For the wages of sin is death, but the free gift of
> God is eternal life in Christ Jesus our Lord. (Rom.
> 6:23)

That price was death, and if it were not paid, it would result in eternal death and separation from God forever.

> But of the tree of the knowledge of good and evil
> you shall not eat, for in the day that you eat of it
> you shall surely die. (Gen. 2:17)

The first Adam did sin, and the process of death began as seen by Adam's effort to be separated or hidden from God. God was not taken by surprise; He already had a plan of correction that He had worked up in ages past.

> Even as he chose us in him before the foundation
> of the world, that we should be holy and blameless
> before him. In love...(Eph. 1:4)

If the first Adam should fail, God had a "last Adam" who would not fail.

> Thus it is written, "The first man Adam became a
> living being"; the last Adam became a life-giving
> spirit. (1 Cor.15: 45)

That last Adam was God Himself, God the Son. By making man a physical being that could die, God had a plan that He would become a man. This God did when God the Son became incarnate, taking on a body of flesh, born a baby at Bethlehem. When man could not perform, not because of injury, but because of sin, Jesus would come onto the field and take man and woman's place—a perfect substitute. He would die the death; they could not die and still retain a relationship with God. Yes, God's plan was that He Himself would be the redeemer of men and women.

> Knowing that you were ransomed from the futile ways inherited from your forefathers, not with perishable things such as silver or gold, but with the precious blood of Christ, like that of a lamb without blemish or spot. He was foreknown before the foundation of the world but was made manifest in the last times for the sake of you who through him are believers in God, who raised him from the dead and gave him glory, so that your faith and hope are in God. (1 Pet. 1:18–21)

If man were to die the death he owed for sin, he would be separated from God forever. Not only that, but man had no other person to take his place; for the whole human race had the same problem and owed the same price of death.

> For all have sinned and fall short of the glory of God…(Rom. 3:23)

Yes, man was in a dilemma; but God, in His wisdom, again had an answer. Since the fall—Adam and Eve's disobedience—sin has been hereditary, passed on from father to child. This leaves every living person with a sin problem and having death looming in their future. There was no possibility of a substitute, for everyone was involved with the same problem. If God was going to provide a redeemer through the incarnation of His Son, how was He going to do it when the sin problem permeated the human race? Much to the chagrin of us men, it seems the sin problem is passed on through us to our progeny. Eve sinned first but in innocence; she was deceived. Adam chose to follow Eve willingly. To avoid having Jesus contaminated with sin in His incarnation, God chose for Jesus to receive His humanity from His mother. Jesus was conceived by the Holy Spirit, not by a human father.

> But as he (Joseph) considered these things, behold, an angel of the Lord appeared to him in a dream, saying, "Joseph, son of David, do not fear to take Mary as your wife, for that which is conceived in her is of the Holy Spirit..." (Matt. 1:20)

This was foretold early in Genesis 3:15 (King James Version) when God pronounced a curse on the serpent (Satan).

> And I will put enmity between thee and the woman, and between thy seed and her seed; it shall bruise thy head, and thou shalt bruise his heel

Continuous conflict was predicted between the hordes of Satan and the woman's seed, which has come to pass in all continuing ages in the spiritual warfare that we are involved in. "Her seed" involves two interesting thoughts: It is normal to speak of the human seed as coming from men, but here it comes from a woman. It is also normal to speak of seed when it involves people to speak of seed in the plural. In two ways, this is not the normal and thus speaks of only one person—a special person—who can be none other than the Lord Jesus Christ. Jesus getting His humanity from His mother did not receive a sin nature in his incarnation and was without sin.

> For we do not have a high priest who is unable to sympathize with our weaknesses, but one who in every respect has been tempted as we are, yet without sin (Heb. 4:15 English Standard Version). Being without sin, Jesus did not have a death price hanging over His head and was thus able to be a substitute and redeemer for others.

Satan and his hordes had a choice; they could obey God or go their own way. We also have a choice; we can choose God's way by accepting His plan of redemption through Jesus or go our own way. Satan acted in pride and lost everything. We can humble ourselves, admit we should have been on the cross rather than Jesus, and by so doing look forward for an eternity of God's richest blessings.

In warfare, it is not unusual to parachute troops into enemy territory in order to gain a stronghold. It seems that this is what God did with Adam in placing him in enemy territory. Man was to lead the effort to put down Satan and return creation to God's rule. Adam failed. The perfect man, the God-man, the Lord Jesus, has not failed and will not fail.

CREATION   CHAP. 4

We have discussed the fact that God created two orders of personal beings—angels and humans. The Bible specifically tells us of the details and time of the creation of man. It was on the sixth day of creation.

> Then God said, "Let us make man in our image, after our likeness. And let them have dominion over the fish of the sea and over the birds of the heavens and over the livestock and over all the earth and over every creeping thing that creeps on the earth." So God created man in his own image, in the image of God he created him; male and female he created them. And God blessed them. And God said to them, "Be fruitful and multiply and fill the earth and subdue it, and have dominion over the fish of the sea and over the birds of the heavens and over every living thing that moves on the earth." And God said, "Behold, I have given you every plant yielding seed that is on the face of all the earth, and every tree with seed in its fruit. You shall have them for food. And to every beast of the earth and to every bird of the heavens and to

> everything that creeps on the earth, everything that
> has the breath of life, I have given every green plant
> for food." And it was so. And God saw everything
> that he had made, and behold, it was very good.
> And there was evening and there was morning, the
> sixth day. (Gen. 1:26–31)

The Bible is clear that the angels were created and that some of them turned from God; however, a definite time is not given. We do know certain things: both the creation and fall of angels had to be before Genesis 3—when fallen Satan tempted Eve.

> Now the serpent was more crafty than any beast
> of the field that the Lord God had made. He said
> to the woman, "Did God actually say, 'You shall
> not eat of any tree in the garden'?" And the woman
> said to the serpent, "We may eat of the fruit of the
> trees in the garden, but God said, 'You shall not eat
> of the fruit of the tree that is in the midst of the
> garden, neither shall you touch it, lest you die.'"
> But the serpent said to the woman, "You will not
> surely die. For God knows that when you eat of it
> your eyes will be opened, and you will be like God,
> knowing good and evil." So when the woman saw
> that the tree was good for food, and that it was
> a delight to the eyes, and that the tree was to be
> desired to make one wise, she took of its fruit and
> ate, and she also gave some to her husband who
> was with her, and he ate. (Gen. 3:1–6)

Don't be deceived that this was only a snake talking. Satan indwelt this creature that Eve was familiar with to enhance the possibility of her falling for his tempting.

From Genesis 1:3 to 2:25 the account of the creation for and of man is given with no mention of Satan or angels. This leaves only Genesis 1:1–2 in the biblical account for the creation and fall of angels. Genesis 1:1 speaks of the creation of the heavens and the earth and is the only place left in scriptures for the creation of angels. This being true, the only place in scripture where Satan's fall could have occurred is in Genesis 1:2. This seems to be further borne out by the fact that "darkness was over the face of the deep." It has already been suggested that the earth in its original form was covered with frozen water or ice. Ice in our solar system and throughout the universe is not uncommon. Satan would cause the emphasis on darkness, not God. This being the case, we conclude that creation explained in Genesis 1:1 must have preceded the six-day account explained in the remainder of Genesis 1 and 2.

The young Earth theorists do not accept this possibility. They say Genesis 1:1 and the six days of creation occurred at the same time. Many of these young Earthers hold to the creation dating of James Ussher (1581–1656), Primate of All Ireland. Ussher used the chronologies of the Bible and other ancient history sources to date the time of Earth's creation as 4004 BC. Others who hold to a young Earth allow for possible gaps in the biblical chronologies but still say the earth is very young—no more than six to ten thousand years old. They say that allowing for anything earlier is only to capitulate to the evolutionist and to allow for great periods of time needed to allow the development of life proposed by the theories of evolution. Evolution, however, is not the reason for believing in a creation of the heavens and the earth before the six-day account. The reason explained here is the existence of angels and the fall of Satan. Job 38:7 clearly states that the angels were there when God laid the foundations of the earth that Job stood on—the same Earth that Adam and Eve stood on and also the same Earth you and I stand on.

There are those who hold to an early creation of the universe and discount evolution as even being a tenable possibility for the development of life. The reasons to discount evolution are various, including the following: (1) the world is an integrated system with the parts depending on each other for continuing existence; (2) the fossil record contains no intermediate phases of life's development, which causes a person to conclude such phases never existed; (3) there is no evidence that great lengths of time result in progress, but rather time results in decay and death, not life; (4) evolution provides no explanation of the initial cause of the material universe; and (5) there is a myriad of other reasons to doubt evolution as a viable explanation of existence and life. The reason for saying the creation of Genesis 1:1 and the six days of creation did not occur at the same time is not evolution but the existence of angels and the fall of Satan.

Let's take a look at the universe. We will begin with our— Milky Way Galaxy. It is estimated that our galaxy is between 100,000– 120,000 light-years in diameter (one light-year is approximately six trillion miles). Think about that! If we'd be traveling at sixty miles per hour continuously, it would take nearly two million years to go one light-year; our galaxy is huge. From data received from the Hubble Space Telescope and Voyager 1 and 2, it is estimated that the universe contains more than one thousand galaxies. When one comes to an end of the sight distances of these telescopes, there appears to still be more out and beyond. The young Earthers say that God could have done all this a few thousand years ago. No one questions that; nothing is impossible with God. The real issue is, *Did He do it all a few thousand years ago?* Is it reasonable to look at the vastness of the universe, and consider that God is eternal, and then say he just started doing things a few thousand years ago?

There is one more issue that some of those who accept only a young earth hold. When asked what God was doing before the creation, they say it is not an issue because God is not limited by time. In saying this, they seem to insinuate that time is only existent to the time man is on this earth. It is true that God is not limited by time, but that is no reason to say time only exists during this age. Mass, space, and time are accepted as fundamental physical quantities that govern the universe. If this is true, time came into being with creation and will continue to exist in the new earth and new heavens. Eternity is not a period when time does not exist, but rather when time is without limits. Limiting time to our present age is not a proof of a young earth. It seems that God has measured time in days (morning and evening) only during this age. It appears there will be no mornings or evenings in the New Jerusalem or in the new earth but just one long, continuous day.

> And the city has no need of sun or moon to shine on it, for the glory of God gives it light, and its lamp *is* the Lamb. By its light will the nations walk, and the kings of the earth will bring their glory into it, and its gates will never be shut by day—and *there will be no night there.* (Rev. 21:23–25)

This does not speak of no time in eternity, but rather of infinite time. A proof of time in eternity is Revelation 22:1–2a.

> Then the angel showed me the river of the water of life, bright as crystal, flowing from the throne of God and of the Lamb, through the middle of the street of the city; also, on either side of the river, the tree of life with its twelve kinds of fruit, yielding its fruit each month…

Months are a measure of time, and we are told there will be twelve months in heaven. Our God will accomplish everything He set out to do. His paradise for man in the "Garden of Eden" was disrupted by sin. This does not mean He has given up on a paradise for believers in His forever family. The new paradise of the New Jerusalem and the New Earth will over shadow Eden. God is not One who changes, and He had time existing in Eden, which is a good reason to believe there will be time in eternity. Why shouldn't there be lots of time; it will take awhile to get acquainted with all of God's saints.

If you are confused about time in eternity, join the throng. It seems songwriters are not agreed on this issue. John Newton (1725–1807), who wrote "Amazing Grace" agrees that there will be lots of time in heaven. He wrote:

> When we've been there *ten thousand years,*
> Bright shining as the sun,
> We've no less days to sing God's praise,
> than when we first begun.

In contrast J. M. Black, who wrote "When the Roll is Called Up Yonder," wrote these words:

When the trumpet of the Lord shall sound
and *time shall be no more*, And the morning
breaks eternal bright and fair—When the
Saved of earth shall gather over on the other shore,
And the roll is called up yonder—I'll be there!

As explained earlier, the old Earthers rely heavily on the fossil record to explain their theories—that the development of the earth took lots of time. We have already shown that their doctrine of uniformitarianism is no explanation for the development of fossils. Sudden burial, not uniform conditions, is required for the development of fossils. In some cases the old earthers hold to the existence of pre-Adamic life to explain their ideas of the fossil record. This theory has no real evidence to support it. The fossil record they depend on heavily can be better explained as we will do in chapter 6. The fossils found around the world are best explained as resulting from the creatures created by God during the six days of creation. Another problem with this theory is the issue of death. Death is caused by sin, and only possible among physical beings and creatures. The Bible says death started with Adam, never before his time in pre-Adamic creatures.

> Therefore, just as sin came into the world through one man, and death through sin, and so death spread to all men because all sinned—for sin indeed was in the world before the law was given, but sin is not counted where there is no law. Yet death reigned from Adam until Moses, even over those whose sinning was not like the transgression of Adam, who was a type of the one who was to come. (Rom. 5: 12–14)

> For if, because of one man's trespass, death reigned through that one man, much more will those who receive the abundance of grace and the free gift of righteousness reign in life through the one man Jesus Christ. (Rom. 5:17)

Now let us explain the support for an early pre-Adamic creation and a young-Earth creation. Today, the predominant view in science for the beginning of the universe is the Big Bang theory. Much of the thinking of this view grew out of efforts to reach the moon. In order to complete an orbit of the moon, the exact location of the moon had to be determined at the time of the arrival of the space capsule.

Physicists calculated forward for the location of the moon so the interception could be made. Using the same principle, they have also traced back into time past and came to the conclusion that the universe had its beginning at one point. Not having an explanation for the cause of the universe's beginning, they theorized that at one time all the materials of the universe were compressed into a capsule, which exploded into the universe that we see today. Although they offer no cause for the capsule or for its explosion, there does seem to be some truth in their findings. The Bible would agree that the universe had a beginning and started from a single point. The difference would be the exploding capsule. I am no astrophysicist, but I have been told that such a concentration of power in a small capsule would not result in our universe, but would rather result in a black hole.

A far better explanation of the universe's beginning is that given by the Bible. There was no capsule, but the omnipotent God spoke the universe into being.

> By the word of the Lord the heavens were made, and by the breath of his mouth all their host. He gathers the waters of the sea as a heap; he puts the deeps in storehouses. Let all the earth fear the Lord; let all the inhabitants of the world stand in awe of him! For he spoke, and it came to be; he commanded, and it stood firm. (Ps. 33:6–9)

> By faith we understand that the universe was created by the word of God, so that what is seen was not made out of things that are visible. (Heb. 11:3)

In these verses, we are given the cause and source of the power that brought our universe into being, which the Big Bang does not offer. Neither is Genesis 1:1 an explanation of a creation that took six days. The creation described in Genesis 1:1 took place in an instant. Astrophysicists say that the first fraction of a second of creation had to be very exact, or we would not have the universe we see today. If the force had been too strong, the materials that constitute our universe would still be flying away. If the force had been too small, the force of gravity would cause everything to collapse back into its place of origin.

God spoke and the universe came into being. We often hear the term creation ex nihilo used today. This is in no way a description of biblical creation. When you start with nothing, do you know what you get? Nothing. The Bible's correct explanation of creation was seen above in the use of Hebrews 11:3. Something that is not visible is not necessarily nothing. And that is the case here. So what is this invisible stuff that the universe is made of? It would be a good idea to let the Bible tell us the answer.

> It is he (God) who made the earth by his power, who established the world by his wisdom, and by his understanding stretched out the heavens. (Jer. 10:12)

> "It is I (God) who by my great power and my outstretched arm have made the earth, with the men and animals that are on the earth, and I give it to whomever it seems right to me...." (Jer. 27:5)

> Ah Lord God! It is you who have made the heavens and the earth by your great power and by your outstretched arm! Nothing is too hard for you. (Jer. 32:17)

It is He (God) Who made the earth by His power, who established the world by His wisdom. And by His understanding, He stretched out the heavens. How did God make the heavens and the earth? It was by His great power—power that is not visible but, at the same time, is not nothing.

Many in the world of science reject the Bible and say it is not scientific. It is true that the Bible is not a book on science; however, it often speaks of areas concerning science. What the Bible says about scientific issues is always true and accurate. We have an example here in dealing with creation. I believe everyone would accept Einstein as a true scientist. Einstein said there was a relationship between energy or power and mass or physical material. We know about his equation, which is stated as:

$$E = MC^2$$
Energy = mass x the speed of light squared

This is exactly what the Bible is saying; God created the universe by His power (energy). The universe is vast and contains a great deal of mass, but this posed no problem to our omnipotent God, whose power is without limit. It does not seem that God's speaking the heavens and earth (universe) into being is a description of the six days of creation. This is another support of an older universe that was originally super-intended by angels.

But is this all true? Do we have any evidence that the universe was formed this way? Where is all the power that was necessary to form the material universe to be what it is today? Well, it is all locked up in the materials of the universe. Split the atom and you have a release of power, a big explosion. Two evidences of this are: first, the nuclear bombs (two atomic bombs released during World War II wiped out two cities in Japan—Nagasaki, and Hiroshima); second, the collision of solar bodies. In science, the Roche limit holds that two bodies of any size will never collide; for the gravitational force of the larger body will take the smaller body apart before collision. In some cases, whole smaller bodies do impact the larger body as evidenced by the craters on earth, on other planets, and on solar bodies throughout the universe. An instance when fragmenting occurred was in early 2013 in central Russia. A body headed for the earth exploded, and the fragments did damage over a large area. This is proof that power is locked up in material substance.

Today, scientists are still at a loss as to why the atom does not fly apart as electrons orbit the nucleus. They don't know, but the Bible has an answer.

> He (Christ) is the image of the invisible God, the firstborn of all creation. For by him all things were created, in heaven and on earth, visible and invisible, whether thrones or dominions or rulers or authorities—all things were created through him and for him. And he is before all things, and in him all things hold together. (Col. 1:15–17)

However, one of these days, He will take His hands off of things; and there will be a great explosion.

> But the day of the Lord will come like a thief, and then the heavens will pass away with a roar, and the heavenly bodies will be burned up and dissolved, and the earth and the works that are done on it will be exposed. Since all these things are thus to be dissolved, what sort of people ought you to be in lives of holiness and godliness, waiting for and hastening the coming of the day of God, because of which the heavens will be set on fire and dissolved, and the heavenly bodies will melt as they burn! (2 Pet. 3:10–12)

Jesus is the only answer for the holy conduct and godliness God requires in the verses above, and He has a great promise for those who turn to Him and trust Him.

> But according to his promise we are waiting for new heavens and a new earth in which righteousness dwells. (2 Pet. 3:13)

Yes, the universe is old. How old, we do not know. But being created by a God, who is eternal, it could be very old. Having said this, I need to say, "I hold the same position as those who hold to a young Earth if we are talking about the present condition of the earth." the only difference in my opinion is that during the six days of creation, God refurbished the earth as it is today in order to support physical life. The earth as we know it is only a few thousand years old—maybe six thousand to ten thousand years old. Life as we know it—whether it be plant, animal, or human—had its beginning during the six days of God's work explained in Genesis 1 and 2. There was no death in the physical realm until after Adam's sin. Neither was there fossils, the result of death, which the old Earthers depend on to try and explain their old and long ages.

Think about this: God created the universe in an instant. He took six days to prepare the earth for men and women. This tells me we are very important to God. Knowing this, we need to live lives that will glorify our heavenly Father. A second thought is that Jesus is taking a lot longer than six days to prepare a heavenly home for us. He left about two thousand years ago to work on it.

> "Let not your hearts be troubled. Believe in God; believe also in me. In my Father's house are many rooms. If it were not so, would I have told you that I go to prepare a place for you? And if I go and prepare a place for you, I will come again and will take you to myself, that where I am you may be also...." (John 14:1–3)

The place that Jesus is preparing is out of this world. He has been working on it for some time, and He was a very good carpenter. Make sure you don't miss it. Make sure you receive Him as your Savior.

Man was God's answer to the sin problem. To begin His work of restoring His creation to perfection, God placed Adam in Satan's realm, where sin had begun. In so doing, the stage was set for the beginning of spiritual warfare. We will look deeper into this issue in the next chapter.

THE FIRST BATTLE   CHAP. 5

Satan is not a dummy. It did not take him very long to realize that this fellow who God placed in his realm was not a friend. When God takes six days to rejuvenate the realm of Satan—so that it would sustain this new creature—God must have a plan that is not to Satan's benefit. Knowing this, Satan set out to win man over to his way of thinking; and he began to look for the right moment for his attack. First, we need to realize that Satan is a coward; he does not fight fair. If what he puts into your mind sounds good, you had better think twice. Being the coward he is, Satan knows his chances of winning are better if he leads his onslaught against the woman.

Not only is Satan a coward, but he is also very patient. Why is this true? Well, look at Adam. God has just given him this raving beauty. How long do you think it was that Adam could not take his eyes off of her, even let her out of his presence? But then one day, the newness wears off; and Adam goes off on his own (just the moment Satan has been waiting for). Knowing that he is a spirit being, and that he might startle Eve and lose a hearing if he approaches her directly, Satan chose to indwell the serpent as he speaks to Eve. To us, today, this would seem to be a bad choice; however, in its original form—until judgment was pronounced upon it by God—the serpent seems to have been one of the most magnificent creatures of God's creation. "Now the serpent was more crafty than any beast of the field which the Lord God had made" (Gen. 3:1).

Satan was ready, and he approaches Eve with the same line of thinking that had caused his own downfall. "God isn't fair. He is holding out on you. Hey, you can be like God!" Eve looked at the tree of the knowledge of good and evil; and sure enough, "it was a delight to the eyes, and that the tree was to be desired to make one wise..." (Gen. 3:6b) Exactly like Satan said, so she thought. So she took and ate and gave some to her husband and he ate. Eve was deceived, but Adam knew what he was doing. He succumbed to the same temptation that has ruined the lives of many men. He chose that chick over God, and things have never been the same. The relationship with God was broken. The walks with God "in the cool of the evening" were over. Ever since, men and women have been running and hiding from God. They have been passing the buck. The man blamed the woman, and the woman blamed the serpent; and God had to pass judgment on all three.

On the serpent:

> The Lord God said to the serpent, "Because you have done this, cursed are you above all livestock and above all beasts of the field; on your belly you shall go, and dust you shall eat all the days of your life...." (Gen. 3:14)

On the woman:

> To the woman he said, "I will surely multiply your pain in childbearing; in pain you shall bring forth children. Your desire shall be for your husband, and he shall rule over you." (Gen. 3:16)

Do you think this Bible stuff is a myth? Try to convince a woman who is about to give birth.

On the man:

> And to Adam he said, "Because you have listened to the voice of your wife and have eaten of the tree of which I commanded you, 'You shall not eat of it,' cursed is the ground because of you; in pain you shall eat of it all the days of your life; thorns and thistles it shall bring forth for you; and you shall eat the plants of the field. By the sweat of your face you shall eat bread till you return to the ground, for out of it you were taken; for you are dust, and to dust you shall return." (Gen. 3:17–19)

Adam brought it on himself (sweat and weeds), but he also brought it on everyone who would follow him. This is a lesson for us. When we sin, we not only hurt ourselves; but we also hurt many others.

So, Satan won the first battle, but God had an answer. His answer is the same: redemption. We saw it first in Genesis 3:15, the seed of the woman. In Genesis 3:21, we see another picture (the skins of animals). It is stated as follows: "The Lord God made garments of skin for Adam and his wife, and clothed them." This is the first shedding of blood in scripture, and it is added to our knowledge of redemption; Jesus had to shed His blood (die) to save us.

In the next step of judgment, Adam and Eve are expelled from the Garden of Eden ("Paradise Lost"). Can paradise be restored? Remember: God always has an answer.

WARFARE CONTINUES   CHAP. 6

After overcoming Adam and Eve with his temptation, Satan must have been very pleased with himself and well on his way to take over for God. He had seen them expelled from their plush estate and camped out among the thorns and tares. He probably felt he had no worries; then Eve begin to have children, and God's earlier words must have haunted him.

> And I (God) will put enmity between thee and
> the woman, and between thy seed and her seed; it
> shall bruise thy head, and thou shalt bruise his heel.
> (Gen. 3:15 King James Version)

Could this woman's seed (children) be his enemies? Thinking they must be enemies, Satan renews his warfare.

CAIN AND ABEL

Watching the first two sons, Satan must have concluded he and the oldest had a lot in common; however the younger worried him, for he thought like God.

> By faith Abel offered to God a more acceptable sac-
> rifice than Cain, through which he was commended
> as righteous, God commending him by accepting
> his gifts. And through his faith, though he died, he
> still speaks. (Heb. 11:4 English Standard Version)

Satan must have thought Abel must go, and he begins to work on Cain's pride and self-sufficiency. When God accepted Abel's offering and not Cain's, it was more than Cain could tolerate; and his anger erupted.

> And the Lord had regard for Abel and his offer-
> ing, but for Cain and his offering he had no regard.
> So Cain was very angry, and his face fell. (Gen.
> 4:4b–5)

From that time on, Cain waited for the day to be rid of his brother. We are told when that day came.

> And when they were in the field, Cain rose up
> against his brother Abel and killed him. (Gen. 4:8b)

Satan won another victory.

Cain had opportunity to seek forgiveness, but he refused and departed from the presence of God.

> Then Cain went away from the presence of the
> Lord and settled in the land of Nod, east of Eden.
> Cain knew his wife, and she conceived and bore
> Enoch. When he built a city, he called the name
> of the city after the name of his son, Enoch. (Gen.
> 4:16–17)

With the increase of his descendants, Cain built a city; and a progressive culture developed. We see the fast development of the arts and sciences. There were advances in music, animal husbandry, and metallurgy (Gen. 4:20–22). But there was no mention of God, and the society became corrupt.

God always has his representative on earth, and the birth of Seth again increased Satan's anxiety.

> And Adam knew his wife again, and she bore a son and called his name Seth, for she said, "God has appointed for me another offspring instead of Abel, for Cain killed him." To Seth also a son was born and he called his name Enosh. At that time people began to call upon the name of the Lord. (Gen. 4:25–26)

With Seth and his descendants, the human race was sharply divided between those who had no place for God in their lives and those who called upon God. With these two lines, there was a sharp division in the human race. With the increase of Seth's descendants and men calling on the Lord, Satan must have become a bit uneasy and began to plan an attack on the Godly line.

SONS OF GOD AND DAUGHTERS OF MEN

Satan's plan was to corrupt the godly line (The Seed of the Woman, Gen. 3:15). By having some of his demon workers cohabit with women, he could corrupt the human race.

> When man began to multiply on the face of the land and daughters were born to them, the sons of God saw that the daughters of man were attractive. And they took as their wives any they chose. (Gen. 6:1–2)

In chapter 2, we identified the sons of God in the Old Testament as angels. Here, the sons of God are fallen angels (demons), who have turned from God to join Satan. By developing a hybrid race of part angel and part human, Satan could so corrupt the human race and make it impossible for the birth of a pure and holy Messiah. There would be no possibility of the plan of redemption being carried out, and the human race would be destroyed. The Bible calls these hybrids

Nephilim. The Nephilim were on the earth in those days, and also afterward, when the sons of God came in to the daughters of man and they bore children to them. These were the mighty men who were of old, the men of renown. (Gen. 6:4)

Satan may have been pleased with the result of his plan, but the Lord was not.

> The Lord saw that the wickedness of man was great in the earth, and that every intention of the thoughts of his heart was only evil continually. And the Lord regretted that he had made man on the earth, and it grieved him to his heart. So the Lord said, "I will blot out man whom I have created from the face of the land, man and animals and creeping things and birds of the heavens, for I am sorry that I have made them." (Gen. 6:5–7)

At this point, God set out for a plan of attack against the hordes of destruction who had followed Satan. A major concern was that it appeared God was vastly outnumbered since only one man (Noah) had remained faithful to God.

> But Noah found favor in the eyes of the Lord....
> Noah was a righteous man, blameless in his gener-
> ation. Noah walked with God. (Gen. 6:8, 9b)

Should numbers have been a concern? Not at all. One with God is always a majority.

God shared with Noah His concern about the increase of violence on the earth and the need to stop it, but because of the magnitude of the violence, the human race would need to be eliminated. And God said to Noah, "I have determined to make an end of all flesh, for the earth is filled with violence through them. Behold, I will destroy them with the earth...." (Gen. 6:13)

And God said to Noah, "I have a job for you. It will only take one hundred twenty years." What would you have said? It probably would have been "God, you are crazy!" Not Noah, he was quick to obey. Noah did this; he did all that God commanded him. (Gen. 6:22)

Some would say, "How could you worship a God, who would destroy the human race?" This they do not seem to understand—that even in judgment, God is merciful. For one hundred twenty years while Noah was building the ark, they had a chance to repent. That is a long time.

Then the Lord said, "My Spirit shall not abide in man forever, for he is flesh: his days shall be one hundred and twenty years." (Gen. 6:3)

These people must have heard the truth, for Noah preached to them; but they seemed to have scorned him.

If he did not spare the ancient world, but preserved Noah, a herald of righteousness, with seven others, when he brought a flood upon the world of the ungodly...(2 Pet. 2:5)

God gives men and women more than ample time to turn to Him. If they end up facing His judgment, they can blame no one but themselves. Even as the animals came two by two and entered the ark, then Noah and his family, and after the door was closed, they still thought Noah was crazy.

> And Noah and his sons and his wife and his sons' wives with him went into the ark to escape the waters of the flood. Of clean animals, and of animals that are not clean, and of birds, and of everything that creeps on the ground, two and two, male and female, went into the ark with Noah, as God had commanded Noah. And after seven days the waters of the flood came upon the earth. (Gen. 7:7–10)

After the ark door closed, God gave them seven more days to reconsider their decision. Only when they were failing their first swimming lesson did they change their minds about Noah.

GOD'S GREAT VICTORY

God has made promises to believers that He will keep; therefore, those who seek to prevent God from keeping His promises must be removed. In the days of Noah, all were defying God but Noah and his family. We are given the story of God's means of removing all opposition.

> The flood continued forty days on the earth. The waters increased and bore up the ark, and it rose high above the earth. The waters prevailed and increased greatly on the earth, and the ark floated on the face of the waters. And the waters prevailed so mightily on the earth that all the high mountains under the whole heaven were covered. The waters prevailed above the mountains, covering them fifteen cubits deep. And all flesh died that moved on the earth, birds, livestock, beasts, all swarming creatures that swarm on the earth, and all mankind. Everything on the dry land in whose nostrils was the breath of life died. (Gen. 7:17–22)

Thus God blotted out every living thing that was upon the face of the land—from man to animals to creeping things and to birds of the sky—and they were blotted out from the earth, and only Noah was left, together with those that were with him in the ark.

AFTER THE FLOOD

God remembered Noah (Gen. 8:1) and, when the right time came, instructed him to leave the ark (Gen. 8:16–17). Noah stepped off the ark to find a whole new world, a world he had not experienced before. A world that would become the world we know today.

Events During the Flood

After seven days; 40 days & nights of rain promised	Genesis 7:4
Flood begins in Noah's 600th yr. 2nd month, 17th day	Genesis 7:11

Fountains of the deep burst open & floodgates of sky opened	Genesis 7:11
Rain fell 40 days & water increased	Genesis 7:12
Waters increase & ark floats on water surface	Genesis 7:17–18
High mountains covered with 15 cubits of water	Genesis 7:19–20
All flesh that moved on the earth perished	Genesis 7:21–23a
Water prevailed on the earth 150 days	Genesis 7:24
Waters subside	Genesis 8:1
Fountains of the deep & flood-gates of sky closed	Genesis 8:2
Water recedes from earth	Genesis 8:3
Water deceased after 150 days & on 7th month, 17day	
the ark rests on Mt. of Ararat	Genesis 8:4
On 10th month, 1st day; the tops of mountains become visible	
(74 days later, after a total of 224 days)	Genesis 8:5
After another 40 days Noah opens windows of ark; sends	
raven then dove, that returns because of water on earth	Genesis 8:6–9
After 7days sends dove, that returns with olive leaf	Genesis 8:10–11
After another 7days sends dove that does not return	Genesis 8:12
In Noah's 601st yr., 1st month, 1st day; ground surface is dry	Genesis 8:13–14
2nd month 27th day earth was dry	Genesis 8:14
God commands Noah to leave the ark	Genesis 8:15–16

Noah was in the ark 377 days, and when God commanded him to leave the ark, he stepped out into a new world. Let us look at some of the differences:

1. Noah was alone with him family. He was no longer a laughing stock.
2. Only wildlife on the earth was that which came off the ark.
3. There were climatic conditions that changed; Noah had to become accustomed to chilly winds.
4. Topography of the earth had changed; the mountain he was standing on was new to Noah.
5. Sea levels had risen.

Today two major areas of debate are the creation, and the flood. (Was there a universal flood?) We should not be surprised about this. The apostle Peter predicted that this would happen.

> Knowing this first of all, that scoffers will come in the last days with scoffing, following their own sinful desires. They will say, "Where is the promise of his coming? For ever since the fathers fell asleep, all things are continuing as they were from the beginning of creation." For they deliberately overlook this fact, that the heavens existed long ago, and the earth was formed out of water and through water by the word of God, and that by means of these the world that then existed was deluged with water and perished. (2 Pet. 3:3–6)

There are conditions on the earth today that are quite unusual. We will list them and then seek to explain how what we see today may have been caused. They are as follows:

1. Fossil beds that contain similar fossils worldwide
2. Sedimentary rock over 75% of the earth's surface
3. Rise in sea levels (It appears that the areas of the Black and Mediterranean Seas that were once inhabited are now underwater.)

4. Frozen mammoths in northern regions that were frozen so quickly that there was hardly any deterioration of the flesh
5. Evidences of tropical plant life in far north regions
6. Pure ice without any salt five thousand feet below sea level in the Antarctica
7. Possible ark sightings at fourteen thousand feet elevation on Mt. Ararat
8. Marine fossils at elevations of four thousand to seven thousand feet
9. Flood legends in many cultures of the world
10. Deposits of glacial till, drifts, boulders, drumlins, and moraines over vast areas of northern latitudes.

Critics discredit any talk of a universal flood, such as the Bible pictures in the days of Noah; however, their explanation of the items listed above fall short of a good cause for conditions that we see today. We will try to give a good possible explanation of how what we see today may have happened.

Most explanations for conditions on the earth today involve dynamics restricted to the earth itself. Included in explanations are continental plate shifts, overthrusts, plate tectonics, and hydroplate theory. Although all these theories contain degrees of truth, when they are taken together, they do not offer the dynamic that would cause what we see across the entire earth. Forces outside of the earth seem to have been necessary to have caused present conditions on the earth.

Fossil remains in northern latitudes indicate that at one time semi-tropical to tropical conditions once covered the entire earth. A canopy of water vapor surrounding the earth could explain this. This is supported by the biblical creation account.

> And God said, "Let there be an expanse in the midst of the waters, and let it separate the waters from the waters." And God made the expanse and separated the waters that were under the expanse from the waters that were above the expanse. And it was so. And God called the expanse Heaven. (Gen. 1:6–8a)

Waters above the expanse that God called heaven would explain a canopy. The dissipation of the canopy would also explain the forty days of rain on the earth. Forty days of rain would require large volumes of water, which a vapor canopy that caused tropical condition on the earth would provide. The Bible tells us that it had not rained on the earth before this time (Gen. 2:5). A question that must be asked if it had not rained before this time: what caused it to rain at the time of the flood?

If the earth at one time had a universal tropical climate (as shown by the fossil remains of mammoths and other large creatures in the far north), then what caused the sudden freezing of these animals? Freezing occurred so quickly that there was no deterioration of the flesh. Some of these animals were frozen so quickly that they still had the vegetation that they were eating in their mouths. The buildup of snow over millions of years, which is the uniformitarians' theory for the ice age, is hardly an adequate explanation for evidence we see today. Nor do present theories explain pure ice five thousand feet below sea level in the Antarctic.

Other unanswered questions are: (1) What caused the ark to land at an elevation of fourteen thousand feet? (2) How did marine fossils end up at elevation of four thousand to seven thousand feet high? (3) Why are the fossil deposits that are spread across all the continents so similar? (4) How is it that flood legends are common worldwide? (5) What is the best explanation for the glacial deposits spread across northern latitudes?

Forty days of rain is the cause of a lot of water; however, it alone hardy explains all of these questions. The ark was really nothing more than a large piece of driftwood, yet it landed at an elevation of fourteen thousand feet. Rain and floods wash debris to the lowest point. Tides leave driftwood and debris at the high point of the tide. Could tides have been a major cause in shaping the earth's surface during the flood? If so, how can tides of great magnitude be explained?

Average tides today caused by the gravitational forces of the sun and moon are approximately 30 inches, with greater heights reached in fjords in northern latitudes. Tides on the earth are proportional to $1/R^3$, where R is the distance between the centers of the moon and the earth. R would thus equal 230,620 miles and, as stated, tides average 30 inches around the world.

Tidal Gradients	R in Miles	Tide Heights
	5896	28 miles
	18,000	over one mile
	12,000	3.375 miles
	15,000	1.75 miles
	13,500	2.37 miles
		(12,515 feet)

The moon's radius is approximately 1079.6 miles or 0.272 times that of the earth. If a solar body from outer space came in contact with the earth and was the size of the moon, it would have had to come roughly within 13,000 miles of the earth to have caused tides that would have put the ark on Mt. Ararat at an elevation of 14,000 feet. If such a body was of a different size, the distance from the earth to have the same effect on the tides on the earth would vary. The planet Mercury has been suggested as such a body. Today, Mercury is in a serene orbit, which prevents it from being impacted by other solar bodies. Even though this is true, the surface of Mercury is deeply cratered. This may suggest that Mercury has not always been in its present orbit and once was in a location where its surface was scarred from impacts with possible comets and meteors. If this be the case, Mercury, with a radius of 1464 miles, is larger than our moon, which means that Mercury would not need to come as close to Earth as a moon sized object to have the same effect on Earth.

This scenario seems to be borne out by the biblical account. Rain fell for forty days, but the waters prevailed over the earth for one hundred fifty days (Gen. 7:24). This would be explained by the fact that Mercury continued to orbit the earth, causing tides that covered the earth after the rain stopped. This could have happened if Mercury's orbit of the earth was highly elliptical. Once Mercury came to the outer limits of its orbit, near the sun, it was pulled into orbit around the sun, where it is today. If this is what actually occurred, there would have been tides which would have covered the mountaintops (Gen.

7:19–20), and they would have been high enough to lift the ark to its location on Mt. Ararat (Gen. 8:4). Tides would have swept across the continents every twenty-four hours for one hundred fifty days until Mercury was pulled out of its orbit around the earth. Tides of this magnitude would provide answers to several of the earth's geological features. First, it would provide an answer to the fact that seventy-five percent of the earth's surface is covered with sedimentary rock. Every twenty-four hours for one hundred fifty days, a layer of silt and gravel would have been laid down with the passing tide. Pressures would have then hardened these sediments into the layers of sedimentary rock that we see around the earth. Second, this would answer the question of why fossil beds that are very similar in their animal and floral specimens are found all around the earth. The tidal waters would have picked up the bodies of the dead creatures and would have dropped them with silt deposits as the tides went out. Sudden burial would also provide the mechanism for the formation of fossils. This would also explain the fact that similar fossil beds are widely spread over the earth. Third, such tides could have carried marine creatures to high elevations. This would explain the fact that marine fossils are found at elevations from four thousand to seven thousand feet high. Flood legends around the world bear out the fact the flood was universal, not local.

This scenario also gives us better answers for the ice age (which was not an age at all but, more likely, occurred at the time of the flood in the days of Noah). It is known that in our own solar system, some of the planets have moons that are mostly pure ice—ice that is super-cooled. If Mercury at one time had such a moon, this would explain some of the conditions found on the earth. Suppose Mercury had such a moon, and when Mercury went into orbit around the earth, this moon was pulled out of its orbit around Mercury by the gravitational forces of the earth. As the moon was pulled toward the earth, it came within Earth's Roche limit; and the gravitational force of the earth fragmented it. As the fragments of this moon approached Earth, their magnetic charges caused these fragments to be concentrated on the earth's poles. Scientists say this could never have happened; however, they do not know the conditions at the time, and their assumptions are likely wrong since evidences on the earth dictate that something like this did happen.

An occurrence similar to this would explain four things: First, it would explain the instant freezing of mammoths and other large animals found in ice caps in northern latitudes. This would be true since an icy body from outer space would have been supercooling to near absolute zero. Second, it would explain how pure ice could be found five thousand feet below sea level as coring has shown. This could have happened when the tide was out over Antarctica, and the ice fragments dropped into an area below sea level. It should be mentioned that cores not only show pure ice five thousand feet below sea level, but also another five thousand feet of pure ice above sea level. Third, such an ice dump would also give a better explanation of the glacial deposits found across the northern hemisphere. An ice dump of this magnitude would have pushed the large glacial deposits of till and boulders ahead of it, leaving a landscape spread with all kinds of rock and soil deposits. The action of large ice deposits would have also gorged out the ravines, valleys, and lakes that we see today. Fourth, it may have been the ice fragments passing through the vapor canopy that caused the canopy to precipitate and the rain to begin.

If what has been proposed is true, the gravitational forces that would have caused tides of such a magnitude would have also caused great forces on the earth's surface. The earth has been compared to an egg—having a thin crush and a molten center. Forces of this magnitude could have been the cause of the foundations of earth to rupture and the fountains of the deep to burst forth (Gen. 7:11). Also, such forces could have caused a great uplift on the earth's surface that would have caused mountain ranges. The earth has two major mountain ranges. The first raising in the Pacific crest including New Zealand, New Guinea, the Philippine Islands, Japan, Aleutian Islands, Rocky Mountains to the Andes in South America. The second range would begin with the Pyrenees (including the Alps), Mountains of Ararat, Caucasus Mountains, the Hindu Kush, the Himalayas, and extending through Indonesia and the Pacific Islands. The theory is that as a solar body orbited the earth, the gravitational force caused the uplift of a mountain range across the earth. The reason for the two different ranges is that many think there was a shift of the earth's axis. It is thought that this may be the cause of the difference in the locations of the North Pole and magnetic North Pole.

One last issue to be explained is the thought that ocean levels may have raised one hundred to three hundred feet after Noah's flood. The reason for this is that there are indications of people living in the areas of the Black and Mediterranean Seas that are now underwater. The forty days of rain, the fountains of the deep gushing forth, and the melting of the ice dropped from outer space can easily explain this rise.

These circumstances seem to give a better explanation for a universal flood than what has been presented by others up to this time; besides, it is never wise to disagree with the Bible.

THE TOWER OF BABEL

Man could have used the excuse that he had no means for controlling evil during the time before the flood. To alleviate this excuse, God introduced human government when the new generations from Noah developed.

> And for your lifeblood I will require a reckoning:
> from every beast I will require it and from man.
> From his fellow man I will require a reckoning for
> the life of man. "Whoever sheds the blood of man,
> by man shall his blood be shed, for God made man
> in his own image. (Gen. 9:5–6)

Human government has been enforced since it was initiated at the time of Noah. Both Paul and Peter amplify its content in the New Testament (Rom. 13:1–7 and 1 Pet. 2:13–17). Even though God gave men the means for controlling evil after the flood, men continued in their disobedience. Rather than being fruitful, multiplying, and filling the earth as God commanded (Gen. 9:1), they flocked together so that they would not be scattered.

> Now the whole earth used the same language and
> the same words. It came about as they journeyed

east, that they found a plain in the land of Shinar
and settled there. They said to one another, "Come,
let us make bricks and burn them thoroughly."
And they used brick for stone, and they used tar
for mortar. They said, "Come, let us build for ourselves a city, and a tower whose top will reach into
heaven, and let us make for ourselves a name, otherwise we will be scattered abroad over the face of
the whole earth. (Gen. 11:1–4)

After observing the building of the tower, the Lord stepped in to
prevent men from multiplying their evil. He did this by confusing their
language and scattering them abroad over the earth.

The Lord came down to see the city and the tower
which the sons of men had built. The Lord said,
"Behold, they are one people, and they all have the
same language. And this is what they began to do,
and now nothing, which they purpose to do, will
be impossible for them. Come, let Us go down
and there confuse their language, so that they will
not understand one another's speech." So the Lord
scattered them abroad from there over the face of
the whole earth; and they stopped building the city.
Therefore its name was called Babel, because there
the Lord confused the language of the whole earth;
and from there the Lord scattered them abroad
over the face of the whole earth. (Gen. 11:5–9)

Yes, the world is locked in a spiritual war. To this point, God
has answered each of Satan's attacks; but Satan will not give up easily.
We will see this as we continue to look at God's outworking of His
program.

THE CALL OF ABRAHAM   CHAP. 7

After the flood, God told Noah and his sons to be fruitful, multiply, and fill the earth. (Gen. 9:1). From Noah's sons, God's request was fulfilled.

> "Now the sons of Noah who came out of the ark were Shem and Ham and Japheth; and Ham was the father of Canaan. These three were the sons of Noah, and from these the whole earth was populated." (Gen. 9:18–19)

According to the biblical record of Shem's descendants (Gen. 11:10–26), Abram was born 292 years after the flood. During this time, the building of the tower of Babel occurred; and God confused people's language and scattered them over the earth. At the time, because of the human propensity for evil, God chose to call Abram and carry on His plans through him and his descendants. Abram was of the line of Shem. In the prophecy of Genesis 9:26, Shem was associated with the true God who was to be blessed. Shem's line was chosen to be the line from which the Messiah would come and seemed to be the more godly of the three lines that rose from Noah. Even though Abram was nine generations removed from Shem, he must have received some godly influence during his bringing up. God must have seen a heart for Him in Abram when He called him.

Secular history tells us that Ur was a Sumerian city-state in ancient Mesopotamia. Some feel that at Abram's time, it may have been the largest city in the world; it had an estimated population of 65,000. Although Ur seems to have had an advanced culture, there seemed to be little knowledge of the true God. During this time, some of the rulers were deified. Temples to the gods were built, including a ziggurat (possibly similar to the Tower of Babel); and the moon god, Nannar, was worshipped.

We are not sure what caused Terah to take his family and move from Ur to go north to Haran. Could it have been that he, being a Shemite, had retained enough knowledge of the true God, and that the idolatry in Ur grieved his soul? Was his experience like that of Lot, who lived in Sodom?

> He (God) rescued righteous Lot, oppressed by the sensual conduct of unprincipled men for by what he saw and heard that righteous man, while living among them, felt his righteous soul tormented day after day by their lawless deeds. (2 Pet. 2:7–8)

There are those who say this was not the case, and Terah him-self was probably an idolater since it was only after Terah's death that Abram felt free to move on to Canaan.

> Terah took Abram his son, and Lot the son of Haran, his grandson, and Sarai his daughter-in-law, his son Abram's wife; and they went out together from Ur of the Chaldeans in order to enter the land of Canaan; and they went as far as Haran, and set-tled there. The days of Terah were two hundred and five years; and Terah died in Haran. Now the Lord said to Abram, "Go forth from your country, and from your relatives and from your father's house, to the land which I will show you." (Gen. 11:31, 12:1)

We can't be sure what is true, but we can be certain that God was at work to bring Abram to Canaan.

For his obedience, Abram was made the following promises by God:

1. I will make you a great nation.
2. I will bless you and make your name great.
3. You shall be a blessing.
4. I will bless those who bless you, and those who curse you I will curse.
5. And in you all the families of the earth will be blessed.

In calling Abram and his descendants, God had at least three major duties for them to accomplish: First, they would be the vessels through whom He would bring His revelation to men and women. This they accomplished in that all the scriptural writers—with the possible exceptions of Job and Luke—were Jewish. Secondly, through the Jewish line, the Messiah would be born. Thirdly, they were to carry God's truth about salvation to all the people of the world. The Jewish people have not done very well in this third duty. In their pride, they have looked down on Gentiles. Many say that God is finished with the Jews; however, what God starts, He finishes. God never fails. In later chapters, we still will see how God brings the Jews to also accomplish this duty.

Even though he was especially called of God, Abram was very human; and Satan got in his potshots against him. Twice Abram pawned Sarai off as his sister before Pharaoh of Egypt (Gen. 12: 10–19) and Abimelech of Gerar (Gen. 20:1–18). On both occasions, Abram went to these places knowing his life was in danger but went anyway, discounting the promises God had made to him, and even endangering the Messianic line. When Lot was taken captive by the kings of the east, Abram went to rescue him though he was greatly outnumbered. Again God saved him from death. Possibly Abram's greatest failure was when he and Sarai decided to help God out by allowing Abram to have an heir by Sarai's handmaid Hagar. History from that time to the present has been a war between the two lines—that of the true heir, Isaac, and that of Hagar's child, Ishmael.

Throughout his life, God continued to give Abram promises. A disappointing time in Abram's life was when his nephew Lot separated from him to go into the area of Sodom. After this, God gave encouragement in promising Abram the land forever, plus a great number of descendants.

> The Lord said to Abram, after Lot had separated from him, "Now lift up your eyes and look from the place where you are, northward and southward and eastward and westward; for all the land which you see, I will give it to you and to your descendants forever. I will make your descendants as the dust of the earth, so that if anyone can number the dust of the earth, then your descendants can also be numbered. Arise, walk about the land through its length and breadth for I will give it to you. (Gen. 13:14–17)

God then made a covenant with Abram to confirm His promises to give Abram the land.

"On that day the Lord made a covenant with Abram, saying, 'To your descendants I have given this land, from the river of Egypt as far as the great river, the river Euphrates'" (Gen. 15:18)

> To confirm His purposes to Abram, God even changed Abram's name. It was changed from Abram (High father or Exalted father) to Abraham (father of a multitude of nations).
>
> Now when Abram was ninety-nine years old, the Lord appeared to Abram and said to him, "I am God Almighty; Walk before Me, and be blameless. 'I will establish My covenant between Me and you, and I will multiply you exceedingly.' Abram fell on his face, and God talked with him, saying, 'As for Me, behold, My covenant is with you, and you will be the father of a multitude of nations. No longer shall your name be called Abram, but

your name shall be Abraham, for I have made you
the father of a multitude of nations. I will make
you exceedingly fruitful, and I will make nations
of you, and kings will come forth from you. I will
establish My covenant between Me and you and
your descendants after you throughout their generations for an everlasting covenant, to be God to
you and to your descendants after you. I will give
to you and to your descendants after you, the land
of your sojournings, all the land of Canaan, for an
everlasting possession; and I will be their God."
(Gen. 17:1–8)

After faithless efforts to help God by suggesting his head servant,
Eliezer, to be his heir (Gen. 15:2–3), and by having a son by Sarai's
handmaid Hagar, Abraham begins to hear God. Finally, Abraham
trusted God completely; and the miracle child, Isaac, was born in his
parent's old age. Abraham's degree of trust was shown when God tested
him by asking him to sacrifice Isaac. Abraham was prepared to do this,
knowing that if God made him carry through on the test, God would
have to raise Isaac from the dead in order to keep the promise He had
made.

"As it is written, 'A father of many nations have I made you' in the
presence of Him whom he believed, even God, who gives life to the
dead and calls into being that which does not exist" (Rom. 4:17)

To Abraham's further credit, he made sure his son, Isaac, had a
godly wife. He sent his leading servant back to his relatives in Haran for
Isaac's wife, Rebecca (Gen. 24). During Isaac's life, Satan again tried to
end the Messianic line when Esau, the oldest and godless twin, sought
to kill his brother Jacob. Although Esau had little spiritual fiber, Jacob
did give him plenty of reason for his hatred. Jacob had snookered Esau
out of the birthright for a bowl of stew. Later, Jacob deceived his father,
Isaac, into blessing him before Esau. Although Isaac was a melancholy
type, his faith can be seen with his actions toward Jacob. So that Jacob
would not marry among the godless Canaanites (Gen. 28:1), Isaac sent
Jacob to Haran to the household of Rebecca's father to obtain a wife
(Gen. 28:2–5). Isaac, thus, sought to preserve the family of Abraham

but also safeguarded Jacob's life by removing him far from his angry brother, Esau.

Jacob arrived in Paddan Aram and met his mother's family. One of the first people he met was his cousin Rachel, the daughter of his mother's brother Laban. This may well have been a case of love at first sight.

> When Jacob saw Rachel the daughter of Laban his mother's brother, and the sheep of Laban his mother's brother, Jacob went up and rolled the stone from the mouth of the well and watered the flock of Laban his mother's brother. Then Jacob kissed Rachel, and lifted his voice and wept. Jacob told Rachel that he was a relative of her father and that he was Rebecca's son, and she ran and told her father." (Gen. 29:10–12)

Jacob was an expert at deception, but he met his match in his uncle Laban. Jacob offered to labor for Laban for seven years for the hand of Rachel, Laban's youngest daughter; but at the end of the seven years, Laban slipped his oldest daughter Leah into Jacob's tent and requested another seven years of labor for Rachel. At the end of twenty years, Jacob possessed a family by Leah, Rachel, and their two handmaids. In addition, he had acquired great herds and wealth for another six years of labor.

"In this way the man (Jacob) grew exceedingly prosperous and came to own large flocks, and female and male servants, and camels and donkeys" (Gen. 30:43)

As Jacob prospered, Laban's sons became jealous of him. Laban's attitude toward Jacob changed, and God appeared to Jacob, telling him it was time to go home.

> Jacob heard that Laban's sons were saying, 'Jacob has taken everything our father owned and has gained all this wealth from what belonged to our father, and Jacob noticed that Laban's attitude toward him was not what it had been. Then the

> Lord said to Jacob, 'Go back to the land of your
> fathers and to your relatives, and I will be with
> you'" (Gen. 31:1–3)

Jacob had received strict instruction from God, but he also had
two wives. Jacob informed his wives of their father's change of attitude
toward him.

> So Jacob sent word to Rachel and Leah to come
> out to the fields where his flocks were. He said to
> them, "I see that your father's attitude toward me
> is not what it was before, but the God of my father
> has been with me. You know that I've worked for
> your father with all my strength, yet your father
> has cheated me by changing my wages ten times."
> (Gen. 31:4–7)

Next, Jacob told his wives of God's instructions for him to return
home.

> "I am the God of Bethel, where you anointed a
> pillar and where you made a vow to me. Now leave
> this land at once and go back to your native land"
> (Gen. 31:13)

With his wives' agreement, Jacob prepared to return to Canaan.

> Then Rachel and Leah replied, "Do we still have
> any share in the inheritance of our father's estate?
> Does he not regard us as foreigners? Not only has
> he sold us, but he has used up what was paid for
> us. Surely all the wealth that God took away from
> our father belongs to our children and us. So do
> whatever God has told you." Then Jacob put his
> children and his wives on camels, and he drove all
> his livestock ahead of him, along with all the goods
> he had accumulated in Paddan Aram, to go to his
> father Isaac in the land of Canaan. (Gen. 31:14–18)

Satan took a final jab at Jacob as he left Paddan Aram. When Laban got word of Jacob's departure, he set out in hot pursuit.

> "When it was told Laban on the third day that Jacob had fled, then he took his kinsmen with him and pursued him a distance of seven days' journey, and he overtook him in the hill country of Gilead. (Gen. 31:23)

Again God was there to protect Jacob, and warned Laban in a dream not to harm Jacob.

> "God came to Laban the Aramean in a dream of the night and said to him, 'Be careful that you do not speak to Jacob either good or bad.'" (Gen. 31:24)

After some sharp discussion, Laban and Jacob made a covenant between them and departed amiably.

> Then Jacob became angry and contended with Laban; and Jacob said to Laban, "What is my transgression? What is my sin that you have hotly pursued me? Though you have felt through all my goods, what have you found of all your household goods? Set it here before my kinsmen and your kinsmen, that they may decide between us two. These twenty years I have been with you; your ewes and your female goats have not miscarried, nor have I eaten the rams of your flocks. That which was torn of beasts I did not bring to you; I bore the loss of it myself. You required it of my hand whether stolen by day or stolen by night. Thus I was: by day the heat consumed me and the frost by night, and my sleep fled from my eyes. These twenty years I have been in your house; I served you fourteen years for your two daughters and six years for your flock, and you changed my wages ten times. If the God of my father, the God of Abraham, and the fear of Isaac,

had not been for me, surely now you would have sent me away empty-handed. God has seen my affliction and the toil of my hands, so He rendered judgment last night." Then Laban replied to Jacob, "The daughters are my daughters, and the children are my children, and the flocks are my flocks, and all that you see is mine. But what can I do this day to these my daughters or to their children whom they have borne? So now come, let us make a covenant, you and I, and let it be a witness between you and me." Then Jacob took a stone and set it up as a pillar. Jacob said to his kinsmen, "Gather stones." So they took stones and made a heap, and they ate there by the heap. Now Laban called it Jegar-sahadutha, but Jacob called it Galeed. Laban said, "This heap is a witness between you and me this day." Therefore it was named Galeed, and Mizpah, for he said, "May the Lord watch between you and me when we are absent one from the other. If you mistreat my daughters, or if you take wives besides my daughters, although no man is with us, see, God is witness between you and me." Laban said to Jacob, "Behold this heap and behold the pillar which I have set between you and me. This heap is a witness, and the pillar is a witness, that I will not pass by this heap to you for harm, and you will not pass by this heap and this pillar to me, for harm. The God of Abraham and the God of Nahor, the God of their father, judge between us." So Jacob swore by the fear of his father Isaac. Then Jacob offered a sacrifice on the mountain, and called his kinsmen to the meal; and they ate the meal and spent the night on the mountain. Early in the morning Laban arose, and kissed his sons and his daughters and blessed them. Then Laban departed and returned to his place. (Gen. 31:36–55)

God again protected Jacob from danger before he arrived back in Canaan. This was when he met his brother, Esau. Twenty years had passed since they had last seen each other. At that time, Esau was searching for a way to kill Jacob.

> "So Esau bore a grudge against Jacob because of the blessing with which his father had blessed him; and Esau said to himself, 'The days of mourning for my father are near; then I will kill my brother Jacob'" (Gen. 27:41)

Jacob feared his brother and spent a sleepless night. He prayed for God's protection and reminded God of His past promises.

> Deliver me, I pray, from the hand of my brother, from the hand of Esau; for I fear him, that he will come and attack me and the mothers with the children. For You said, 'I will surely prosper you and make your descendants as the sand of the sea, which is too great to be numbered.' (Gen. 32:11–12)

As Jacob cried to the Lord for protection, God met with him; and Jacob wrestled with God. At that time, God made Jacob a promise that has echoed through history to our present day.

> Then he (God) said, "Let me go, for the dawn is breaking." But he (Jacob) said, "I will not let you go unless you bless me." So He said to him, "What is your name?" And he said, "Jacob." He said, "Your name shall no longer be Jacob, but Israel for you have striven with God and with men and have prevailed." (Gen. 32:26–28)

As morning came, Jacob selected a very large present for his brother from his herds in hope of appeasing his brother (Gen. 32:13–15). Jacob's fears did not subside as he saw his brother coming with four hundred men (Gen. 33:1). Next, we see a tremendous example of the effectiveness of prayer as God answered Jacob's prayer of the night before. As Esau approached, Jacob moved ahead of the company with him and bowed to Esau; and God removed Esau's anger.

> "But he (Jacob) passed on ahead of the rest and bowed down to the ground seven times, until he came near to his brother. Then Esau ran to meet him and embraced him, and fell on his neck and kissed him, and they wept" (Gen. 33:3–4)

The brothers departed peacefully: Esau went back to his home in Seir (Gen. 33:16), and Jacob journeyed on to Succoth and pitched his tent before Shechem in the Land of Canaan (Gen. 33:17–18).

ISRAEL BECOMES A NATION, PART I   CHAP. 8

Jacob was back in the Promised Land, but his problems were not over. Why did he stop at Shechem in Succoth? Why did he not go to Bethel, where he had met with God when he was departing for Haran? Why didn't he go to Beersheba, where his father, Isaac, was still alive? We do not know what Jacob was thinking, but later, events proved that it was not a good decision. It was not long before Jacob's children were visiting with the daughters of the land. Shechem, a prince of the land, saw Dinah, Jacob's daughter, and took her by force and raped her. Shechem loved Dinah and asked his father, Hamor, to ask for her hand in marriage.

> Hamor spoke with them (Jacob's sons), saying, "The soul of my son Shechem longs for your daughter; please give her to him in marriage. Intermarry with us; give your daughters to us and take our daughters for yourselves. Thus you shall live with us, and the land shall be open before you; live and trade in it and acquire property in it." Shechem also said to her father and to her brothers, "If I find favor in your sight, then I will give whatever you say to me. Ask me ever so much bridal payment and gift, and

> I will give according as you say to me; but give me
> the girl in marriage." (Gen. 34:8–12)

What a deal! Everything sounded so good, but that is Satan's way. Again it was only another effort to corrupt the Messianic line. Jacob's sons were grieved and answered Shechem and his father, Hamor, with deceit.

> But Jacob's sons answered Shechem and his father
> Hamor with deceit, because he had defiled Dinah
> their sister. They said to them, "We cannot do this
> thing, to give our sister to one who is uncircum-
> cised, for that would be a disgrace to us. Only on
> this condition will we consent to you: if you will
> become like us, in that every male of you be cir-
> cumcised, then we will give our daughters to you,
> and we will take your daughters for ourselves, and
> we will live with you and become one people. But if
> you will not listen to us to be circumcised, then we
> will take our daughter and go." (Gen. 34:13–17)

To most people, this would not sound like much of a deal; but the men of the land had their eyes on Jacob's possessions.

> "Will not their livestock and their property and all
> their animals be ours? Only let us consent to them,
> and they will live with us" (Gen. 34:23)

Jacob's sons' purpose was not to live in harmony with the Shechemites but to avenge their sister for what was done to her.

> Now it came about on the third day, when they
> were in pain, that two of Jacob's sons, Simeon and
> Levi, Dinah's brothers, each took his sword and
> came upon the city unawares, and killed every male.
> They killed Hamor and his son Shechem with the
> edge of the sword, and took Dinah from Shechem's
> house, and went forth. Jacob's sons came upon the

slain and looted the city, because they had defiled
their sister. They took their flocks and their herds
and their donkeys, and that which was in the city
and that which was in the field; and they captured
and looted all their wealth and all their little ones
and their wives, even all that was in the houses.
(Gen. 34:25–29)

Jacob was not pleased with the action of his sons.

Then Jacob said to Simeon and Levi, "You have
brought trouble on me by making me odious
among the inhabitants of the land, among the
Canaanites and the Perizzites; and my men being
few in number, they will gather together against me
and attack me and I will be destroyed, I and my
household." (Gen. 34:30)

Jacob's fear and God's command compelled Jacob to move on
to Bethel, where he belonged; but before moving on, Jacob called for
everyone to purify themselves before the Lord.

Then God said to Jacob, "Arise, go up to Bethel
and live there, and make an altar there to God, who
appeared to you when you fled from your brother
Esau." So Jacob said to his household and to all
who were with him, "Put away the foreign gods
which are among you, and purify yourselves and
change your garments; and let us arise and go up to
Bethel, and I will make an altar there to God, who
answered me in the day of my distress and has been
with me wherever I have gone." (Gen. 35:1–3)

Finally, Jacob had come clean with the Lord; and when he arrived
at Bethel, God was there to bless him. God's blessing to Jacob included
the same promises He had given to Abraham and Isaac.

> Then God appeared to Jacob again when he came from Paddan-aram, and He blessed him. God said to him, "Your name is Jacob; you shall no longer be called Jacob, But Israel shall be your name." Thus He called him Israel. God also said to him, "I am God Almighty; be fruitful and multiply. A nation and a company of nations shall come from you, And kings shall come forth from you. "The land which I gave to Abraham and Isaac, I will give it to you, And I will give the land to your descendants after you." (Gen. 35:9–12)

Having worshipped at Bethel, Jacob moved on toward Ephrath/Bethlehem, approximately ten miles from his father, Isaac, who was still living in Hebron.

> "Jacob came to his father Isaac at Mamre of Kiriath-arba (that is, Hebron), where Abraham and Isaac had sojourned." (Gen. 35:27)

On the way, Rachel, Jacob's favorite wife, died in giving birth to Jacob's twelfth son, Benjamin.

> Now there were twelve sons of Jacob—the sons of Leah: Reuben, Jacob's firstborn, then Simeon and Levi and Judah and Issachar and Zebulun; the sons of Rachel: Joseph and Benjamin; and the sons of Bilhah, Rachel's maid: Dan and Naphtali; and the sons of Zilpah, Leah's maid: Gad and Asher. These are the sons of Jacob who were born to him in Paddan-aram. (Gen. 35:22b–26) From these twelve sons, God would form the nation, Israel. On the surface it appeared that harmony had been restored in Isaac's family. The two brothers were together to bury their father at his death.

> "Now the days of Isaac were one hundred and eighty years. Isaac breathed his last and died and

was gathered to his people, an old man of ripe age; and his sons Esau and Jacob buried him" (Gen. 35:28)

Behind the scenes, things were not as rosy. Jacob's numbers were small, and he was surrounded by the idol-worshipping people of the land. Did they remember what his sons had done at Shechem? There was also the danger of his family mixing with the people of the land. Remember Dinah? Would Jacob's sons be swept away by the beauties of the land?

Yes, there were dangers; and God begin to carry out plans to separate his people from those living in the land. Sadly there would be heartache, deceit, and deep hurt before harmony was again restored. Jealousy arose when Joseph tattled to his father about the bad actions of his brothers. The fact that Joseph was his father's favorite did not help things.

> Joseph, when seventeen years of age, was pasturing the flock with his brothers while he was still a youth, along with the sons of Bilhah and the sons of Zilpah, his father's wives. And Joseph brought back a bad report about them to their father. Now Israel loved Joseph more than all his sons, because he was the son of his old age; and he made him a varicolored tunic. His brothers saw that their father loved him more than all his brothers; and so they hated him and could not speak to him on friendly terms. (Gen. 37:2–4)

The brothers' hatred of Joseph intensified when Joseph told them about two dreams that he had.

> Then Joseph had a dream, and when he told it to his brothers, they hated him even more. He said to them, "Please listen to this dream which I have had; for behold, we were binding sheaves in the field, and lo, my sheaf rose up and also stood erect; and behold, your sheaves gathered around and

bowed down to my sheaf." Then his brothers said
to him, "Are you actually going to reign over us? Or
are you really going to rule over us?" So they hated
him even more for his dreams and for his words.
Now he had still another dream, and related it to
his brothers, and said, "Lo, I have had still another
dream; and behold, the sun and the moon and
eleven stars were bowing down to me." He related
it to his father and to his brothers; and his father
rebuked him and said to him, "What is this dream
that you have had? Shall I and your mother and
your brothers actually come to bow ourselves down
before you to the ground?" His brothers were jealous of him, but his father kept the saying in mind.
(Gen. 37:6–11)

Knowing his sons were pasturing their flocks in Shechem, Jacob
(Israel) was concerned about their welfare and sent Joseph to check
on them. Seeing Joseph coming from a distance, the brothers' anger
erupted; and they began to plot his death.

When they saw him from a distance and before he
came close to them, they plotted against him to
put him to death. They said to one another, "Here
comes this dreamer! Now then, come and let us kill
him and throw him into one of the pits; and we
will say, 'A wild beast devoured him.' Then let us
see what will become of his dreams!" But Reuben
heard this and rescued him out of their hands and
said, "Let us not take his life." Reuben further said
to them, "Shed no blood. Throw him into this pit
that is in the wilderness, but do not lay hands on
him"—that he might rescue him out of their hands,
to restore him to his father. So it came about, when
Joseph reached his brothers, that they stripped
Joseph of his tunic, the varicolored tunic that was
on him; and they took him and threw him into the

> pit. Now the pit was empty, without any water in
> it. (Gen. 37:18–24)

Hardened by their hatred for Joseph, the brothers sat down to eat their lunch while Joseph cried for mercy from the depths of the pit. As they ate, they spotted a caravan of traders passing by. Seeing the caravan, Judah saw an opportunity to make a buck on his brother, which would be better than killing him. The brothers agreed, and Joseph was sold to the traders for twenty pieces of silver; and Joseph landed in Egypt.

> Then they sat down to eat a meal. And as they
> raised their eyes and looked, behold, a caravan of
> Ishmaelites was coming from Gilead, with their
> camels bearing aromatic gum and balm and myrrh,
> on their way to bring them down to Egypt. Judah
> said to his brothers, "What profit is it for us to
> kill our brother and cover up his blood? Come
> and let us sell him to the Ishmaelites and not lay
> our hands on him, for he is our brother, our own
> flesh." And his brothers listened to him. Then some
> Midianite traders passed by, so they pulled him up
> and lifted Joseph out of the pit, and sold him to the
> Ishmaelites for twenty shekels of silver. Thus they
> brought Joseph into Egypt. (Gen. 37:25–28)

After these events, there were few happy times in Israel. The brothers fabricated a lie about Joseph to deceive their father and lived with a perpetually guilty conscience. Israel lived with deep sorrow as he grieved for his son, and efforts to comfort him were largely a failure. Being purchased by Potiphar, the captain of Pharaoh's bodyguard, Joseph landed in the ranks of Pharaoh's court.

> Now Reuben returned to the pit, and behold,
> Joseph was not in the pit; so he tore his garments.
> He returned to his brothers and said, "The boy is
> not there; as for me, where am I to go?" So they
> took Joseph's tunic, and slaughtered a male goat

and dipped the tunic in the blood; and they sent the varicolored tunic and brought it to their father and said, "We found this; please examine it to see whether it is your son's tunic or not." Then he examined it and said, "It is my son's tunic. A wild beast has devoured him; Joseph has surely been torn to pieces!" So Jacob tore his clothes, and put sackcloth on his loins and mourned for his son many days. Then all his sons and all his daughters arose to comfort him, but he refused to be comforted. And he said, "Surely I will go down to Sheol in mourning for my son." So his father wept for him. Meanwhile, the Midianites sold him in Egypt to Potiphar, Pharaoh's officer, the captain of the bodyguard. (Gen. 37:29–36)

Down in Egypt, things were going well for Joseph. Because of his faithful service, Potiphar made him the overseer of his house and all that he owned (Gen. 39:2–6). Satan was still seeking to upset God's plan, and in a short time, Potiphar's wife sought to seduce Joseph. When he refused and ran from her, she accused Joseph of rape; and he landed in the king's prison (Genesis 39:6b–20). Again Joseph was faithful, and God extended kindness to him; and in short order, the chief jailer put Joseph in a supervisory capacity.

But the Lord was with Joseph and extended kindness to him, and gave him favor in the sight of the chief jailer. The chief jailer committed to Joseph's charge all the prisoners who were in the jail; so that whatever was done here, he was responsible for it. The chief jailer did not supervise anything under Joseph's charge because the Lord was with him; and whatever he did, the Lord made to prosper. (Gen. 39:21–23)

Back in the land, it was another story. Intermarriage was occurring with the idol worshippers of the land. To make matters worse for Jacob, Judah was involved with a Canaanite woman.

> And it came about at that time that Judah departed from his brothers and visited a certain Adullamite, whose name was Hirah. Judah saw there a daughter of a certain Canaanite whose name was Shua; and he took her and went in to her. So she conceived and bore a son and he named him Er. Then she conceived again and bore a son and named him Onan. She bore still another son and named him Shelah; and it was at Chezib that she bore him. Now Judah took a wife for Er his firstborn, and her name was Tamar. But Er, Judah's firstborn was evil in the sight of the Lord, so the Lord took his life. Then Judah said to Onan, "Go in to your brother's wife, and perform your duty as a brother-in-law to her, and raise up offspring for your brother." Onan knew that the offspring would not be his; so when he went in to his brother's wife, he wasted his seed on the ground in order not to give offspring to his brother. But what he did was displeasing in the sight of the Lord; so He took his life also. Then Judah said to his daughter-in-law Tamar, "Remain a widow in your father's house until my son Shelah grows up"; for he thought, "I am afraid that he too may die like his brothers." So Tamar went and lived in her father's house. (Gen. 38:1–11)

Although the two sons of Judah, who Tamar had been with, were evil, she saw something in the Israelites she wanted to be a part of; and she waited an opportunity to be a part of Israel. After Judah's wife died (Gen. 38:12), Tamar heard that Judah was passing her way. She dressed as a prostitute; and when Judah passed by, he went into her, promising a goat as payment. As a pledge, she asked for Judah's seal, cord, and staff until payment was made. Tamar then redressed in her widow's garments and was never found so that payment could be made. Three months later, Judah heard that Tamar was pregnant. Assuming it was by harlotry, he was ready to have her burning. But when Tamar produced the items of the pledge, and stated that she was with child by the man to whom these things belong, Judah had to admit that Tamar was more righteous than he was (Genesis 38:12–24). We might question Tamar's methods, but God honored her faith by allowing her to be in the genealogy of the Lord, the line of Messiah. Tamar, his daughter-in-law, bore him (Judah) Perez and Zerah. Judah had five sons in all (1 Chron. 2:4). Judah was the father of Perez and Zerah by Tamar What we learn from this are the following: (1) God wants all people to be saved—even those who have been worshipping idols, (2) Women are not second-rate citizens in God's Kingdom, and (3) For faithfulness, God gives high honors—even to be a mother in the line of Messiah.

Major problems still existed for God's plan for Israel. Not many of the Canaanites would exhibit the faith of Tamar, and the dark cloud of paganism hung over Israel's family. Meanwhile, back in Egypt, God was preparing Joseph for the work ahead. As a supervisor under the chief jailer, Joseph was learning leadership. It seemed Joseph's time had come when two of the king's official servants were put under his charge.

> Then it came about after these things, the cup-bearer and the baker for the king of Egypt offended their lord, the king of Egypt. Pharaoh was furious with his two officials, the chief cupbearer and the chief baker. So he put them in confinement in the house of the captain of the bodyguard, in the jail, the same place where Joseph was imprisoned. The captain of the bodyguard put Joseph in charge of them, and he took care of them; and they were in confinement for some time. Then the cupbearer and the baker for the king of Egypt, who were confined in jail, both had a dream the same night, each man with his own dream and each dream with its own interpretation. When Joseph came to them in the morning and observed them, behold, they were dejected. He asked Pharaoh's officials who were

with him in confinement in his master's house, "Why are your faces so sad today?" Then they said to him, "We have had a dream and there is no one to interpret it." Then Joseph said to them, "Do not interpretations belong to God? Tell it to me, please." (Gen. 40:1–8)

After being told the dreams of the two men, Joseph interpreted them, telling the cupbearer that he would be restored to his position in the king's service, but that the baker would be hanged; then, Joseph asked the cupbearer to remember him before Pharaoh.

Only keep me in mind when it goes well with you, and please do me a kindness by mentioning me to Pharaoh and get me out of this house. For I was in fact kidnapped from the land of the Hebrews, and even here I have done nothing that they should have put me into the dungeon." (Gen. 40:14–15)

Yet the unthankful chief cupbearer, caught in his own affairs, did not remember Joseph. And Joseph languished in prison another two years until Pharaoh had two dreams that bothered him, and upon hearing about Pharaoh's dreams, the cupbearer remembered Joseph.

Now it happened at the end of two full years that Pharaoh had a dream, and behold, he was standing by the Nile. And lo, from the Nile there came up seven cows, sleek and fat; and they grazed in the marsh grass. Then behold, seven other cows came up after them from the Nile, ugly and gaunt, and they stood by the other cows on the bank of the Nile. The ugly and gaunt cows ate up the seven sleek and fat cows. Then Pharaoh awoke. He fell asleep and dreamed a second time; and behold, seven ears of grain came up on a single stalk, plump and good. Then behold, seven ears, thin and scorched by the east wind, sprouted up after them. The thin ears swallowed up the seven plump and full ears. Then

Pharaoh awoke and behold, it was a dream. Now in the morning his spirit was troubled, so he sent and called for all the magicians of Egypt, and all its wise men. And Pharaoh told them his dreams, but there was no one who could interpret them to Pharaoh. Then the chief cupbearer spoke to Pharaoh, saying, "I would make mention today of my own offenses. Pharaoh was furious with his servants, and he put me in confinement in the house of the captain of the bodyguard, both me and the chief baker. We had a dream on the same night, he and I; each of us dreamed according to the interpretation of his own dream. Now a Hebrew youth was with us there, a servant of the captain of the bodyguard, and we related them to him, and he interpreted our dreams for us. To each one he interpreted according to his own dream. And just as he interpreted for us, so it happened; he restored me in my office, but he hanged him." Then Pharaoh sent and called for Joseph, and they hurriedly brought him out of the dungeon; and when he had shaved himself and changed his clothes, he came to Pharaoh. (Gen. 4:1–14)

When Pharaoh asked Joseph if he was able to interpret dreams, Joseph told him it was not in him to interpret dreams, but that God would give Pharaoh a favorable answer; then Pharaoh told Joseph his dreams, and Joseph explained their meaning to Pharaoh.

Now Joseph said to Pharaoh, "Pharaoh's dreams are one and the same; God has told to Pharaoh what He is about to do. The seven good cows are seven years; and the seven good ears are seven years; the dreams are one and the same. The seven lean and ugly cows that came up after them are seven years, and the seven thin ears scorched by the east wind will be seven years of famine. It is as I have spoken to Pharaoh: God has shown to Pharaoh what He is about to do. Behold, seven years of great abundance are coming in all the land of Egypt; and after them seven years of famine will come, and all the abundance will be forgotten in the land of Egypt, and the famine will ravage the land. So the abundance will be unknown in the land because of that subsequent famine; for it will be very severe. Now as for the repeating of the dream to Pharaoh twice, it means that the matter is determined by God, and God will quickly bring it about. Now let Pharaoh look for a man discerning and wise, and set him over the land of Egypt. Let Pharaoh take action to appoint overseers in charge of the land, and let him exact a fifth of the produce of the land of Egypt in the seven years of abundance. Then let them gather all the food of these good years that are coming, and store up the grain for food in the cities under Pharaoh's authority, and let them guard it. Let the food become as a reserve for the land for the seven years of famine which will occur in the land of Egypt, so that the land will not perish during the famine." Now the proposal seemed good to Pharaoh and to all his servants. (Gen. 41:25–37)

Pharaoh followed through on Joseph's recommendation to find a wise man to set over the affairs of Egypt, and said he could find no one better suited for the position than Joseph. What a coincidence! In a matter of minutes, Joseph went from prisoner to ruler over Pharaoh's house. Well, there was really no coincidence here at all! God had planned this all along and was preparing Joseph for this position for the past thirteen years.

Then Pharaoh said to his servants, "Can we find a man like this, in whom is a divine spirit?" So Pharaoh said to Joseph, "Since God has informed you of all this, there is no one so discerning and wise as you are. You shall be over my house, and according to your command all my people shall do homage; only in the throne I will be greater than you." Pharaoh said to Joseph, "See, I have set you over all the land of Egypt." Then Pharaoh took off his signet ring from his hand and put it on Joseph's hand, and clothed him in garments of fine linen and put the gold necklace around his neck. He had him ride in his second chariot; and they proclaimed before him, "Bow the knee!" And he set him over all the land of Egypt. Moreover, Pharaoh said to Joseph, "Though I am Pharaoh, yet without your permission no one shall raise his hand or foot in all the land of Egypt." Then Pharaoh named Joseph Zaphenath-paneah; and he gave him Asenath, the daughter of Potiphera priest of On, as his wife. And Joseph went forth over the land of Egypt. Now Joseph was thirty years old when he stood before Pharaoh, king of Egypt. And Joseph went out from the presence of Pharaoh and went through all the land of Egypt. (Gen. 41:38–46)

In full control, Joseph went to work. During the seven good years, he stored in grain in such abundance that it could not be measured (Gen. 41:49); then the famine came, and Pharaoh put everything into Joseph charge.

When the seven years of plenty which had been in the land of Egypt came to an end, and the seven years of famine began to come, just as Joseph had said, then there was famine in all the lands, but in all the land of Egypt there was bread. So when all the land of Egypt was famished, the people cried out to Pharaoh for bread; and Pharaoh said to all the Egyptians, "Go to Joseph; whatever he says to you, you shall do." When the famine was spread over all the face of the earth, then Joseph opened all the storehouses, and sold to the Egyptians; and the famine was severe in the land of Egypt. The people of all the earth came to Egypt to buy grain from Joseph, because the famine was severe in all the earth. (Gen. 41:53–57)

Soon Joseph's family felt the pangs of the famine in Canaan, and Jacob sent his sons to Egypt for food. Arriving in Egypt, the brothers bowed before Joseph; for they did not recognize him and took him as one of the rulers of Egypt. Joseph recognized his brothers and began testing them by accusing them of being spies. He did this to see if there had been any change in their attitudes over the years.

Now Joseph was the ruler over the land; he was the one who sold to all the people of the land. And Joseph's brothers came and bowed down to him with their faces to the ground. When Joseph saw his brothers he recognized them, but he disguised himself to them and spoke to them harshly. And he said to them, "Where have you come from?" And they said, "From the land of Canaan, to buy food." But Joseph had recognized his brothers, although they did not recognize him. Joseph remembered the dreams which he had about them, and said to them, "You are spies; you have come to look at the undefended parts of our land." (Gen. 42:6–9)

Joseph then put them in prison three days before allowing them to return home. Joseph held Simeon hostage and told them to return only if they brought their youngest brother, Benjamin, who was not with them. If they did this, he would know they were not spies. The harsh treatment was working as the brother's conscience caused them to confess their guilt.

Then they said to one another, "Truly we are guilty concerning our brother, because we saw the distress of his soul when he pleaded with us, yet we would not listen; therefore this distress has come

> upon us." Reuben answered them, saying, "Did I
> not tell you, 'Do not sin against the boy'; and you
> would not listen? Now comes the reckoning for his
> blood." They did not know, however, that Joseph
> understood, for there was an interpreter between
> them. He turned away from them and wept. But
> when he returned to them and spoke to them, he
> took Simeon from hem and bound him before
> their eyes. (Gen. 42:21–24)

The famine was severe, and Joseph's family was again in need of
food. Reluctantly, Jacob finally allowed the brothers to return to Egypt
with Benjamin. When Joseph saw Benjamin, he instructed his house
steward to prepare for his brothers to dine with him. After dining,
Joseph sent his brothers home but had his steward put his silver cup in
Benjamin's bag. After the men departed, Joseph sent his steward after
them to retrieve the cup and to question them for doing evil and to
return them to the city. When the brothers returned, Joseph said the
one in whose sack the cup was found would be his slave and would
remain in Egypt. At this point, Judah pled to be a slave in place of
Benjamin. He did this in order to not cause his father, Jacob, more
grief when Benjamin did not return.

Seeing that his brothers were repentant for their past actions,
Joseph asked to be alone with them so he could reveal his true identity
to them.

> Then Joseph said to his brothers, "Please come
> closer to me." And they came closer. And he said,
> "I am your brother Joseph, whom you sold into
> Egypt. Now do not be grieved or angry with your-
> selves, because you sold me here, for God sent me
> before you to preserve life. (Gen. 45:4–5)

When Pharaoh heard that Joseph's brothers had come, he told
Joseph to invite them to bring their household and return to live in
Egypt.

> Now when the news was heard in Pharaoh's house that Joseph's brothers had come, it pleased Pharaoh and his servants. Then Pharaoh said to Joseph, "Say to your brothers, 'Do this: load your beasts and go to the land of Canaan, and take your father and your households and come to me, and I will give you the best of the land of Egypt and you will eat the fat of the land.' Now you are ordered, 'Do this: take wagons from the land of Egypt for your little ones and for your wives, and bring your father and come. Do not concern yourselves with your goods, for the best of all the land of Egypt is yours.'" Then the sons of Israel did so; and Joseph gave them wagons according to the command of Pharaoh, and gave them provisions for the journey. (Gen. 45:16–21)

Jacob was stunned to hear that Joseph was alive. When his spirit was revived, he offered sacrifices of gratitude to God and made ready to go see his son. God's plan to keep his people in Israel safe and to preserve the Messianic line was being fulfilled. Jacob and his family were being welcomed to Egypt in safety.

> Now these are the names of the sons of Israel, Jacob and his sons, who went to Egypt: Reuben, Jacob's firstborn. The sons of Reuben: Hanoch and Pallu and Hezron and Carmi. The sons of Simeon: Jemuel and Jamin and Ohad and Jachin and Zohar and Shaul the son of a Canaanite woman. The sons of Levi: Gershon, Kohath, and Merari. The sons of Judah: Er and Onan and Shelah and Perez and Zerah (but Er and Onan died in the land of Canaan). And the sons of Perez were Hezron and Hamul. The sons of Issachar: Tola and Puvvah and Iob and Shimron. The sons of Zebulun: Sered and Elon and Jahleel. These are the sons of Leah, whom she bore to Jacob in Paddan-aram, with his daugh-

ter Dinah; all his sons and his daughters numbered thirty-three. The sons of Gad: Ziphion and Haggi, Shuni and Ezbon, Eri and Arodi and Areli. The sons of Asher: Imnah and Ishvah and Ishvi and Beriah and their sister Serah. And the sons of Beriah: Heber and Malchiel. These are the sons of Zilpah, whom Laban gave to his daughter Leah; and she bore to Jacob these sixteen persons. The sons of Jacob's wife Rachel: Joseph and Benjamin. Now to Joseph in the land of Egypt were born Manasseh and Ephraim, whom Asenath, the daughter of Potiphera, priest of On, bore to him. The sons of Benjamin: Bela and Becher and Ashbel, Gera and Naaman, Ehi and Rosh, Muppim and Huppim and Ard. These are the sons of Rachel, who were born to Jacob; there were fourteen persons in all. The sons of Dan: Hushim. The sons of Naphtali: Jahzeel and Guni and Jezer and Shillem. These are the sons of Bilhah, whom Laban gave to his daughter Rachel, and she bore these to Jacob; there were seven persons in all. All the persons belonging to Jacob, who came to Egypt, his direct descendants, not including the wives of Jacob's sons, were sixty-six persons in all, and the sons of Joseph, who were born to him in Egypt were two; all the persons of the house of Jacob, who came to Egypt, were seventy. (Gen. 46:8–27)

Joseph went out to meet his father, Jacob, and then gave instruction for them when they met Pharaoh.

When Pharaoh calls you and says, 'What is your occupation?' You shall say, 'Your servants have been keepers of livestock from our youth even until now, both we and our fathers,' that you may live in the land of Goshen; for every shepherd is loathsome to the Egyptians." (Gen. 46:33–34)

When Joseph's brothers met Pharaoh, they did as instructed; and he allowed them to live in the rich land of Goshen and even asked them to be in charge of his livestock. Being shepherds, they became loathsome to the Egyptians, which prevented opportunities for inter-marriage. Israel was now in a place of safety and in an environment that prevented them from marrying the people of the land. They were ready to begin the growth into a nation.

> "Now Israel lived in the land of Egypt, in Goshen, and they acquired property in it and were fruitful and became very numerous (Gen. 47:27)

> After Joseph died the Israelites continued to multiply until the new Pharaoh became fearful of their numbers. But the sons of Israel were fruitful and increased greatly, and multiplied, and became exceedingly mighty, so that the land was filled with them. Now a new king arose over Egypt, who did not know Joseph. He said to his people, "Behold, the people of the sons of Israel are more and mightier than we. Come, let us deal wisely with them, or else they will multiply and in the event of war, they will also join themselves to those who hate us, and fight against us and depart from the land." So they appointed taskmasters over them to afflict them with hard labor. And they built for Pharaoh storage cities, Pithom and Raamses. But the more they afflicted them, he more they multiplied and the more they spread out, so that they were in dread of the sons of Israel. (Exod. 1:7–12)

Next, in order to stop the increase of Israelite population, Pharaoh ordered that all baby boys born to Israelites must be cast into the Nile. But God used Pharaoh's evil plan to prepare and train the future deliverer of His people from Egypt.

> Now a man from the house of Levi went and married a daughter of Levi. The woman conceived and

bore a son; and when she saw that he was beautiful, she hid him for three months. But when she could hide him no longer, she got him a wicker basket and covered it over with tar and pitch. Then she put the child into it and set it among the reeds by the bank of the Nile. His sister stood at a distance to find out what would happen to him. The daughter of Pharaoh came down to bathe at the Nile, with her maidens walking alongside the Nile; and she saw the basket among the reeds and sent her maid, and she brought it to her. When she opened it, she saw the child, and behold, the boy was crying. And she had pity on him and said, "This is one of the Hebrews' children." Then his sister said to Pharaoh's daughter, "Shall I go and call a nurse for you from the Hebrew women that she may nurse the child for you?" Pharaoh's daughter said to her, "Go ahead." So the girl went and called the child's mother. Then Pharaoh's daughter said to her, "Take this child away and nurse him for me and I will give you your wages." So the woman took the child and nursed him. The child grew, and she brought him to Pharaoh's daughter and he became her son. And she named him Moses, and said, "Because I drew him out of the water." (Exod. 2:1–10)

Thus Moses ended up in the king's court and received the best training possible in his day.

"Moses was educated in all the learning of the Egyptians, and he was a man of power in words and deeds (Acts 7:22)

Something about his early days when his mother nursed him for Pharaoh's daughter must have stuck with Moses, for when he was grown, he turned from his Egyptian training.

> By faith Moses, when he had grown up, refused to be called the son of Pharaoh's daughter, choosing rather to endure ill-treatment with the people of God than to enjoy the passing pleasures of sin, considering the reproach of Christ greater riches than the treasures of Egypt; for he was looking to the reward. (Heb. 11:24–26)

Moses wanted to be identified with God's people, but he got ahead of God. There was a day when he went out to visit his brethren, and seeing an Egyptian beating a Hebrew, Moses killed the Egyptian. When Moses heard that Pharaoh knew of the incident and sought to kill Moses, Moses fled to Midian. There, God left Moses on the shelf until He was ready to use Moses.

ISRAEL BECOMES A NATION, PART II   CHAP. 9

Forty years had come and passed. Moses had taken a wife and had two sons. He kept busy in Midian, caring for his father-in-law's flocks. Back in Egypt, conditions were not so serene. The king had died, but for the children of Israel, things had only gotten worse.

> And the sons of Israel sighed because of the bondage, and they cried out; and their cry for help because of their bondage rose up to God. So God heard their groaning; and God remembered His covenant with Abraham, Isaac, and Jacob. God saw the sons of Israel, and God took notice of them. (Exod. 2:23–25)

The day came, as Moses was pasturing the flocks, when the angel of the Lord appeared to him and explained conditions back in Egypt.

> The Lord said, "I have surely seen the affliction of My people who are in Egypt, and have given heed to their cry because of their taskmasters, for I am aware of their sufferings. So I have come down to deliver them from the power of the Egyptians, and to bring them up from that land to a good and spa-

cious land, to a land flowing with milk and honey, to the place of the Canaanite and the Hittite and the Amorite and the Perizzite and the Hivite and the Jebusite. Now, behold, the cry of the sons of Israel has come to Me; furthermore, I have seen the oppression with which the Egyptians are oppressing them. (Exod. 3:7–9)

The Lord told Moses that he was sending him to Pharaoh so that he could bring his people out of Egypt. Moses expressed great doubt about his ability and questioned the Lord. Finally, after being thoroughly instructed by the Lord and given signs to convince Pharaoh, Moses took leave from his father-in-law and reluctantly left for Egypt. The Lord called Aaron to meet his brother Moses in the wilderness. Arriving back in Egypt, they went to the elders of the people of Israel to explain to them the words of the Lord to Moses.

Now the Lord said to Aaron, "Go to meet Moses in the wilderness." So he went and met him at the mountain of God and kissed him. Moses told Aaron all the words of the Lord with which He had sent him, and all the signs that He had commanded him to do. Then Moses and Aaron went and assembled all the elders of the sons of Israel; and Aaron spoke all the words, which the Lord had spoken to Moses. He then performed the signs in the sight of the people. So the people believed; and when they heard that the Lord was concerned about the sons of Israel and that He had seen their affliction, then they bowed low and worshiped. (Exod. 4:27–31)

After this, Moses and Aaron went to Pharaoh to carry out their mission.,

"Thus says the Lord, the God of Israel, 'Let My people go that they may celebrate a feast to Me in the wilderness.'" But Pharaoh said, "Who is the Lord that I should obey His voice to let Israel go?

I do not know the Lord, and besides, I will not let
Israel go" (Exod. 5:1–2)

Pharaoh got a big laugh out of this, for in those days, it was
believed that the great nations had the greatest gods. Who were these
slave people who were asking favors of him? Surely, their god was very
insignificant. So instead of hearing Moses and Aaron, he increased the
workload required of the Israelites.

Pharaoh was soon to learn that it does not pay to challenge the
true God, the God of Israel. Under the increased workload, the Israelites
cried out; and Moses went to God, saying that confronting Pharaoh
had only brought harm to his people. And God reminded Moses of His
covenant promised to Israel and His promised deliverance.

> God spoke further to Moses and said to him, "I
> am the Lord; and I appeared to Abraham, Isaac,
> and Jacob, as God Almighty, but by My name,
> Lord, I did not make Myself known to them. I
> also established My covenant with them, to give
> them the land of Canaan, the land in which they
> sojourned. Furthermore I have heard the groan-
> ing of the sons of Israel, because the Egyptians are
> holding them in bondage, and I have remembered
> My covenant. Say, therefore, to the sons of Israel, 'I
> am the Lord, and I will bring you out from under
> the burdens of the Egyptians, and I will deliver you
> from their bondage. I will also redeem you with an
> outstretched arm and with great judgments. (Exod.
> 6:2–6)

Pharaoh told Moses and Aaron that he did not know the God of
Israel and had no reason to let Israel go. He was about to learn more
about the God of Israel than he ever wanted to know. Challenge God
and guess who wins. Spiritual warfare was about to burst out in full
fury, for God sent His team back to confront Pharaoh with the following instructions:

> Then the Lord said to Moses, "See, I make you as God to Pharaoh, and your brother Aaron shall be your prophet. You shall speak all that I command you, and your brother Aaron shall speak to Pharaoh that he let the sons of Israel go out of his land. But I will harden Pharaoh's heart that I may multiply My signs and My wonders in the land of Egypt. When Pharaoh does not listen to you, then I will lay My hand on Egypt and bring out My hosts, My people the sons of Israel, from the land of Egypt by great judgments. The Egyptians shall know that I am the Lord, when I stretch out My hand on Egypt and bring out the sons of Israel from their midst." (Exod. 7:1–5)

As the battle raged, Pharaoh's men matched the signs of God. Just as Jannes and Jambres opposed Moses, so have these men opposed the truth—men of depraved minds, rejected in regard to the faith (2 Timothy 3:8). Pharaoh's wise men matched God's signs for a time but soon found themselves powerless before God. When they told Pharaoh they could not match the power of God, he would not hear.

> The magicians tried with their secret arts to bring forth gnats, but they could not; so there were gnats on man and beast. Then the magicians said to Pharaoh, "This is the finger of God." But Pharaoh's heart was hardened, and he did not listen to them, as the Lord had said. (Exod. 8:18–19)

God warned Pharaoh when Aaron's rod turned into a serpent. When Pharaoh turned a deaf ear to Moses and Aaron, God began His battle, which raged through ten plagues:

1. Nile turns to blood.
2. Frogs cover the land of Egypt.
3. Gnats spread throughout Egypt.
4. Flies fill the houses in Egypt.
5. Pestilence hit the livestock in Egypt.

6. Boils break out on men and beasts.
7. Hail falls on men, beasts, and plants.
8. Locusts cover the surface of the whole land.
9. Darkness covers the land for three days.
10. Death consumes every firstborn man and beast in the land.

With the land of Egypt devastated and with Pharaoh brought to his knees, God was ready to lead His people out of slavery and form them into a nation. Even Pharaoh consented.

> Then he (Pharaoh) called for Moses and Aaron at night and said, "Rise up, get out from among my people, both you and the sons of Israel; and go, worship the Lord, as you have said. Take both your flocks and your herds, as you have said, and go, and bless me also. (Exod. 12:31–32)

Also, the people of Egypt begged Israel to leave and gladly gave them what they asked for their journey. It seems there were Egyptians with great insight that recognized that the God of Israel was greater than the gods of Egypt, for it is told that a mixed multitude left Egypt with Israel.

> The Egyptians urged the people, to send them out of the land in haste, for they said, "We will all be dead."...Now the sons of Israel had done according to the word of Moses, for they had requested from the Egyptians articles of silver and articles of gold, and clothing; and the Lord had given the people favor in the sight of the Egyptians, so that they let them have their request. Thus they plundered the Egyptians. Now the sons of Israel journeyed from Rameses to Succoth, about six hundred thousand men on foot, aside from children. A mixed multitude also went up with them, along with flocks and herds, a very large number of livestock. (Exod. 12:32–37)

About six hundred thousand men left Egypt, and—counting women and children—it is estimated that between two and three million people all told were in the departing group. Our God knows the hearts of men. First of all, he knew the hearts of the Israelites that should they go directly into the Promised Land and see war, they might desire to return to Egypt. Knowing this, God led them on His chosen route through the wilderness.

> Now when Pharaoh had let the people go, God did not lead them by the way of the land of the Philistines, even though it was near; for God said, "The people might change their minds when they see war, and return to Egypt. "Hence God led the people around by the way of the wilderness to the Red Sea; and the sons of Israel went up in martial array from the land of Egypt. (Exod. 13:17–18)

Don't think that Pharaoh really had a change of heart. He soon realized his slave workforce was gone, and he set out in hot pursuit. God was way ahead of Pharaoh and placed the Israelites in position for Pharaoh's attack.

> Now the Lord spoke to Moses, saying, "Tell the sons of Israel to turn back and camp before Pi-hahiroth, between Migdol and the sea; you shall camp in front of Baal-zephon, opposite it, by the sea. For Pharaoh will say of the sons of Israel, 'They are wandering aimlessly in the land; the wilderness has shut them in.' Thus I will harden Pharaoh's heart, and he will chase after them; and I will be honored through Pharaoh and all his army, and the Egyptians will know that I am the Lord." And they did so. (Exod. 14:1–4)

As the army of Pharaoh approached with horses and chariots, the Israelites, filled with fear, were ready to turn on Moses and return to Egypt.

> But Moses said to the people, "Do not fear! Stand by and see the salvation of the Lord, which He will accomplish for you today; for the Egyptians whom you have seen today, you will never see them again forever. The Lord will fight for you while you keep silent." (Exod. 14:13–14)

As Moses quieted the people, God gave the final battle instructions, a plan to permanently end Egypt's domination of Israel.

> Then the Lord said to Moses, "Why are you crying out to Me? Tell the sons of Israel to go forward. As for you, lift up your staff and stretch out your hand over the sea and divide it, and the sons of Israel shall go through the midst of the sea on dry land. As for Me, behold, I will harden the hearts of the Egyptians so that they will go in after them; and I will be honored through Pharaoh and all his army, through his chariots and his horsemen. Then the Egyptians will know that I am the Lord, when I am honored through Pharaoh, through his chariots and his horsemen." (Exod. 14:15–18)

Without knowledge or relationship with the true God, the Egyptians were dupes for God's trap.

> Then the Egyptians took up the pursuit, and all Pharaoh's horses, his chariots and his horsemen went in after them into the midst of the sea. At the morning watch, the Lord looked down on the army of the Egyptians through the pillar of fire and cloud and brought the army of the Egyptians into confusion. He caused their chariot wheels to swerve, and He made them drive with difficulty; so the Egyptians said, "Let us flee from Israel, for the Lord is fighting for them against the Egyptians." Then the Lord said to Moses, "Stretch out your hand over the sea so that the waters may come

back over the Egyptians, over their chariots and their horsemen." So Moses stretched out his hand over the sea, and the sea returned to its normal state at daybreak, while the Egyptians were fleeing right into it; then the Lord overthrew the Egyptians in the midst of the sea. The waters returned and covered the chariots and the horsemen, even Pharaoh's entire army that had gone into the sea after them; not even one of them remained. (Exod. 14:23–28)

God's plan for His people to be a nation was on course, not to be hindered by outside nations.

Thus the Lord saved Israel that day from the hand of the Egyptians, and Israel saw the Egyptians dead on the seashore. When Israel saw the great power which the Lord had used against the Egyptians, the people feared the Lord, and they believed in the Lord and in His servant Moses. (Exod. 14:30–31)

What is your take on what you have just read? Critics would say that this is a nice story but only a myth that is not supported by secular history. But is the critical view correct? Libraries are full of information about the Exodus. It's true that much of what is written is from a Jewish point of view and not from Egyptian records; however, in all human history, has a nation put forth an effort to report its defeats? Certainly mighty Pharaoh was not going to allow it to be recorded that he was made a mockery by his slaves. Josephus, a credible scholar, even gives the number of chariots, horsemen, and infantrymen.

At this point, I would like to include two recent reports that seem to verify the Exodus. It is true that these accounts have not been seen in secular news, but that is usually the case with any information that supports the truth of the Bible. The first report is that of fossilized chariot wheels and cabs with fossilized skeletal remains of horses and soldiers being found in the Gulf of Aqaba. A reason for critics to question the biblical account of the crossing of the Red Sea is that the crossing was thought to be adjacent to the east side of Egypt in the area of the present-day Suez Canal. In this area, there would be no need of a sea crossing because of a continuous land mass. Since the Gulf of Aqaba is considered to be a northern extension of the Red Sea, a sea crossing in this area would not be unreasonable. This would also agree with the Bible record that the crossing was of the Red Sea. We have already seen another support for this area in that God was leading them to a point where the defeat of the Egyptians would take place. Hence God led the people around by the way of the wilderness to the Red Sea; and the sons of Israel went up in martial array from the land of Egypt. (Exod. 13:17–18)

Another support of this finding is that dating tests of the fossilized remains say that they date from the time of the Exodus.

A second report that supports the Exodus is satellite information from the Iraq war. During the war, Saddam Hussein had positioned his tanks then camouflaged and partially buried them to hide them from aerial surveillance. At this point, America shifted its Keyhole satellite into position over the Iraqi desert. With infrared scanners able to defect temperature difference of only half a degree, the camouflaged tanks could be located; however, the satellite found more than tanks. As the satellite photo was turned toward Egypt, a thin, red line was discovered running eastward from the Nile Delta across the Sinai Peninsula and dropping down to the Gulf of Aqaba, the northeasternmost finger of the Red Sea. The thin, red line seemed to mark the route of the Exodus, but what caused the line to appear on satellite photos?

When the Gulf War finally ended, archaeologists went back into the region to discover how it was possible for a 3,500-year-old trail to exist well enough to show up on satellite photos. They found that two to three million people, with all their livestock, pulverized the desert sand into a fine powder. During the desert nights, the humidity rises to levels near one hundred percent, thus, wetting the powdery sand, making a concrete-like substance. Through the years, the highway was buried by shifting sands, protecting the trail from the elements. During the day, it would heat up like the Iraqi tanks; and being denser than the surrounding sand, it would continue holding the heat longer into the cold nights! The infrared scanners picked up the temperature differential and clearly marked the path of The Exodus. A coincidence? There are no coincidences with God. An interesting 3,500-year-old prophecy in Exodus 9:16 states: "But indeed for this purpose I have raised you up, that I may show my power in you, and that my name may be declared in all the earth." This historical event of 3,500 years ago has, indeed, been declared in all the earth just as the ancient prophecy said it would.

It took God a matter of days in removing Pharaoh's opposition to His plan to make Israel a nation. Dealing with His own people would require God to take a greater amount of time. While God was preparing Israel to become a nation, giving them the Law needed for a nation (Exod. 25–31) and a form of worship, making plans for the tabernacle (Exod. 25–31), and supervising its construction (Exod. 26–40), Israel was excelling in grumbling. They grumbled early on because of lack of water (Exod. 15:24). For lack of meat, they said it would have been better to have died in Egypt (Exod. 16:3). And again because of lack of water, they quarreled with Moses (Exod. 17:2–3). The Israelites could have excused their disobedience by saying, "We have been a slave people. We do not know what the Lord expects of us." In giving Israel the law, God clearly detailed His expectation for them both as individuals and as a nation. If Israel heard God and obeyed His voice, God promised that they would be His special people. Israel emphatically agreed with what God said.

> Now then, if you will indeed obey My voice and keep My covenant, then you shall be My own possession among all the peoples, for all the earth is Mine; and you shall be to Me a kingdom of priests and a holy nation. These are the words that you (Moses) shall speak to the sons of Israel. So Moses came and called the elders of the people, and set before them all these words, which the Lord had commanded him. All the people answered together and said, "All that the Lord has spoken we will do!" (Exod. 19:5–8a)

Although the Israelites were quick to agree with God in word, their hearts and actions did not change. To top off their disobedience and lack of trust in God, they built and worshipped a golden calf (Exod. 32:1–30). At this point, even God was ready to depart from the disobedient Israelites; and He told Moses to go along without Him.

> Go up to a land flowing with milk and honey; for I will not go up in your midst, because you are an obstinate people, and I might destroy you on the way. (Exod. 33:3)

Only Moses' intercession caused God to continue with Israel on the journey to the Promised Land.

> "Now therefore, I pray You, if I have found favor in Your sight, let me know Your ways that I may know You, so that I may find favor in Your sight. Consider too, that this nation is Your people." And He said, "My presence shall go with you, and I will give you rest." Then he said to Him, "If Your presence does not go with us, do not lead us up from here. For how then can it be known that I have found favor in Your sight, I and Your people? Is it not by Your going with us, so that we, I and Your people, may be distinguished from all the other people who are upon the face of the earth?" (Exod. 33:13–16)

After the Law had been given, and the construction of the tabernacle was complete, the Lord's glory filled the tabernacle; and the Lord again led Israel.

> Then the cloud covered the tent of meeting, and the glory of the Lord filled the tabernacle. Moses was not able to enter the tent of meeting because the cloud had settled on it, and the glory of the Lord filled the tabernacle. Throughout all their journeys whenever the cloud was taken up from over the tabernacle, the sons of Israel would set out; but if the cloud was not taken up, then they did

> not set out until the day when it was taken up. For throughout all their journeys, the cloud of the Lord was on the tabernacle by day, and there was fire in it by night, in the sight of all the house of Israel. (Exod. 40:34–38)

One year, one month, and twelve days had passed since the Israelites had left Egypt. Preparations were complete; all had been done for Israel to become a nation. The only thing needed now was for them to be in their own land, the land God had promised to their forefathers, Abraham, Isaac and Jacob. God was ready to lead them to the place that had long been promised.

> Now in the second year, in the second month, on the twentieth of the month, the cloud was lifted from over the tabernacle of the testimony; and the sons of Israel set out on their journeys from the wilderness of Sinai. Then the cloud settled down in the wilderness of Paran. So they moved out for the first time according to the commandment of the Lord through Moses. (Num. 10:11–13)

> Thus they set out from the mount of the Lord three days' journey, with the ark of the covenant of the Lord journeying in front of them for the three days, to seek out a resting place for them. The cloud of the Lord was over them by day when they set out from the camp. Then it came about when the ark set out that Moses said, "Rise up, O Lord! And let your enemies be scattered, and let those who hate you flee before you." When it came to rest, he said, "Return, O Lord, to the myriad thousands of Israel." (Num. 10:33–36)

Although the Lord was ready to lead the people, the Israelites had not had a change of heart and were still complaining and looking back to Egypt.

> Now the people became like those who complain of adversity in the hearing of the Lord; and when the Lord heard it, His anger was kindled, and the fire of the Lord burned among them and consumed some of the outskirts of the camp. The people therefore cried out to Moses, and Moses prayed to the Lord and the fire died out. So the name of that place was called Taberah, because the fire of the Lord burned among them. The rabble who were among them had greedy desires; and also the sons of Israel wept again and said, "Who will give us meat to eat? We remember the fish, which we used to eat free in Egypt, the cucumbers and the melons and the leeks and the onions and the garlic, but now our appetite is gone. There is nothing at all to look at except this manna." (Num. 11:1–6)

Even Moses' own family—Aaron and Miriam—spoke out against Moses.

> Then Miriam and Aaron spoke against Moses because of the Cushite woman whom he had married (for he had married a Cushite woman); and they said, "Has the Lord indeed spoken only through Moses? Has He not spoken through us as well?" And the Lord heard it…. So the anger of the Lord burned against them and He departed. But when the cloud had withdrawn from over the tent, behold, Miriam was leprous, as white as snow…. So Miriam was shut up outside the camp for seven days, and the people did not move on until Miriam was received again. (Num. 12:1–2, 9–10, 15)

When things quieted down, the Lord was again ready to move toward the Promised Land. Afterward, the people moved out from Hazeroth and camped in the wilderness of Paran (Exod. 12:16); and the Lord asked Moses to select spies—one from each of the twelve tribes—to go into the land He was going to give them and bring back a report of their findings.

> Then the Lord spoke to Moses saying, "Send out for yourself men so that they may spy out the land of Canaan, which I am going to give to the sons of Israel; you shall send a man from each of their fathers' tribes, everyone a leader among them." So Moses sent them from the wilderness of Paran at the command of the Lord, all of them men who were heads of the sons of Israel. (Exod. 13:1–3)

In spite of God's marvelous workings among the people—deliverance from Egypt, destroying of Pharaoh's pursuing army, provision in the desert for several million people and their livestock—the people continued to give more heed to the enemy of men's souls then to their God. Giving no heed to God's promise to give them a land flowing with milk and honey, the spies brought back a divided report.

> When they returned from spying out the land, at the end of forty days, they proceeded to come to Moses and Aaron and to all the congregation of the sons of Israel in the wilderness of Paran, at Kadesh; and they brought back word to them and to all the congregation and showed them the fruit of the land. Thus they told him, and said, "We went in to the land where you sent us; and it certainly does flow with milk and honey, and this is its fruit. Nevertheless, the people who live in the land are strong, and the cities are fortified and very large; Amalek is living in the land of the Negev and the Hittites and the Jebusites and the Amorites are living in the hill country, and the Canaanites are living by the sea and by the side of the Jordan." Then Caleb quieted the people before Moses and said, "We should by all means go up and take possession of it, for we will surely overcome it." But the men

who had gone up with him said, "We are not able to go up against the people, for they are too strong for us." So they gave out to the sons of Israel a bad report of the land which they had spied out, saying, "The land through which we have gone, in spying it out, is a land that devours its inhabitants; and all the people whom we saw in it are men of great size. There also we saw the Nephilim (the sons of Anak are part of the Nephilim); and we became like grasshoppers in our own sight, and so we were in their sight." (Num. 13:25–33)

Rather than considering how the Lord had provided, and without hearing what Caleb and Joshua said about the good in the land and the ability of the Israelites to take it, the people only heard the report of the ten who said that the people in the land were too many and too big to be taken. The people were even ready to return to Egypt.

Then all the congregation lifted up their voices and cried, and the people wept that night. All the sons of Israel grumbled against Moses and Aaron; and the whole congregation said to them, "Would that we had died in the land of Egypt! Or would that we had died in this wilderness! Why is the Lord bringing us into this land, to fall by the sword? Our wives and our little ones will become plunder; would it not be better for us to return to Egypt?" So they said to one another, "Let us appoint a leader and return to Egypt." (Num. 14:1–4)

The obstinacy of the people caused the Lord to think about starting over again and making a nation from Moses. Only the intercession of Moses kept God's plan on track. Moses, more than any person, understood the glory of God and what the nations would say if He could not control His own people.

The Lord said to Moses, "How long will this people spurn Me? And how long will they not believe in

Me, despite all the signs which I have performed in their midst? I will smite them with pestilence and dispossess them, and I will make you into a nation greater and mightier than they." But Moses said to the Lord, "Then the Egyptians will hear of it, for by Your strength You brought up this people from their midst, and they will tell it to the inhabitants of this land. They have heard that You, O Lord, are in the midst of this people, for You, O Lord, are seen eye to eye, while Your cloud stands over them; and You go before them in a pillar of cloud by day and in a pillar of fire by night. Now if You slay this people as one man, then the nations who have heard of Your fame will say, 'Because the Lord could not bring this people into the land which He promised them by oath, therefore He slaughtered them in the wilderness.' But now, I pray, let the power of the Lord be great, just as You have declared, the Lord is slow to anger and abundant in loving kindness, forgiving iniquity and transgression; but He will by no means clear the guilty, visiting the iniquity of the fathers on the children to the third and the fourth generations.' Pardon, I pray, the iniquity of this people according to the greatness of Your loving-kindness, just as You also have forgiven this people, from Egypt even until now." (Num. 14:11–19)

The Lord heard the intercession of Moses, but He laid down conditions for His going on before the people. None of the people who had put Him to the test would enter the land. They would wander in the wilderness for forty years—one year for each day the spies were in the land.

So the Lord said, "I have pardoned *them* according to your word; but indeed, as I live, all the earth will be filled with the glory of the Lord. Surely all the men who have seen My glory and My signs which I performed in Egypt and in the wilderness, yet have put Me to the test these ten times and have not listened to My voice, shall by no means see the land which I swore to their fathers, nor shall any of those who spurned Me see it. But My servant Caleb, because he has had a different spirit and has followed Me fully, I will bring into the land, which he entered, and his descendants shall take possession of it. The Lord spoke to Moses and Aaron, saying, "How long *shall I bear* with this evil congregation who are grumbling against Me? I have heard the complaints of the sons of Israel, which they are making against Me. Say to them, 'As I live,' says the Lord, 'just as you have spoken in My hearing, so I will surely do to you; your corpses will fall in this wilderness, even all your numbered men, according to your complete number from twenty years old and upward, who have grumbled against Me. Surely you shall not come into the land in which I swore to settle you, except Caleb the son of Jephunneh and Joshua the son of Nun. Your children, however, whom you said would become a prey—I will bring them in, and they will know the land, which you have rejected. But as for you, your corpses will fall in this wilderness. Your sons shall be shepherds for forty years in the wilderness, and they will suffer *for* your unfaithfulness, until your corpses lie in the wilderness. According to the number of days, which you spied out the land, forty days, for every day you shall bear your guilt a year, *even* forty years, and you will know My opposition. I, the Lord, have spoken, surely this I will do to all this evil congregation who are gathered together against Me. In this wilderness they shall be destroyed, and there they will die.'" (Num. 14:20–24, 26–35)

For disobedience, those who spoke against the Lord were condemned to wander in the wilderness until they perished for forty long years. The only uncertainty was: whose funeral would be next? The Lord began slowly but surely to remove those who spoke against him, and yet contention continued.

1. Those involved in the rebellion of Korah with their family were swallowed up alive as the earth opened up. (Num. 16:1–25)
2. Grumbling against Moses and Aaron resulted in a plague in which 14,700 died. (Num. 16:41–50)
3. Contention over lack of water (Num. 20:2–8)
4. When the people complained about the manna and lack of water, the Lord sent fiery serpents among them and many died. (Num. 21:4–9)
5. Israelites played the Harlot with the daughters of Moab, and a plague killed 24,000. (Numbers 25:1-9)

In spite of Israel's disobedience, God gave success with victories east of the Jordan River.

1. Victory over the Canaanite, King of Arad (Num. 21:1–4)
2. Victory over the Amorites (Num. 21:21–31)
3. Victory over Bashan (Num. 21:33–34)
4. Victory over the Midianites (Num. 31:1–12)

With these victories, further preparations were made to cross the Jordan and the entering of the Promised Land. Joshua was commissioned to replace Moses (Num. 27:15–23). The tribes of Reuben, Gad, and half the tribe of Manasseh were allowed to settle on the east side of the Jordan on the condition that the men from these tribes would cross the Jordan with the remaining tribes to help take the land (Num. 32:1–42). Moses, coming to the end of his time of leadership, gave instructions for possessing the land (Num. 33:50–56). Moses reminded them that they had originally agreed to keep the Lord's commandments.

Now that they were ready to enter the land, it was necessary to continue keeping the Lord's commandments so that it would be well with them, and that their days in the land would be prolonged. In addition to his instructions, Moses gave them a formula that would result in them multiplying greatly in the land, a commandment that he had received from the Lord.

> The Lord heard the voice of your words when you spoke to me, and the Lord said to me, 'I have heard the voice of the words of this people which they have spoken to you. They have done well in all that they have spoken. Oh that they had such a heart in them, that they would fear Me and keep all My commandments always, that it may be well with them and with their sons forever! Go; say to them, "Return to your tents." But as for you, stand here by Me, that I may speak to you all the commandments and the statutes and the judgments which you shall teach them, that they may observe them in the land which I give them to possess.' So you shall observe to do just as the Lord your God has commanded you; you shall not turn aside to the right or to the left. You shall walk in all the way which the Lord your God has commanded you, that you may live and that it may be well with you, and that you may prolong your days in the land which you will possess. (Deut. 5:28–33)

> Now this is the commandment, the statutes and the judgments which the Lord your God has commanded me to teach you, that you might do them in the land where you are going over to possess it, so that you and your son and your grandson might fear the Lord your God, to keep all His statutes and His commandments which I command you, all the days of your life, and that your days may be prolonged. O Israel, you should listen and be careful

to do it, that it may be well with you and that you
may multiply greatly, just as the Lord, the God of
your fathers, has promised you, in a land flowing
with milk and honey. (Deut. 6:1–3)

Moses went on to remind the Israelites of a principle their forefathers had not heeded, and they needed to consider as they came into
the land a principle that men of all ages have largely ignored. A principle we today have given little heed to that is bringing peril to our world
today. The principle is as follows: Pay attention to and be thankful for
what you have, and do not be consumed by what you do not have. The
Israelites had forgotten their great deliverance from slavery and the
Lord's care and provision in the wilderness, and therefore considered
often about returning to Egypt. How much more fruitful would life
be if we were thankful for what we have, and would stop allowing all
our energies to be wasted by fretting over what we do not have? The
Israelites were coming into a land with great provisions that were not
the result of any effort on their part. Moses questions, "How will they
react?" Would they be true to the Living God, who had given them so
much?

"Then it shall come about when the Lord your God
brings you into the land which He swore to your
fathers, Abraham, Isaac and Jacob, to give you,
great and splendid cities which you did not build,
and houses full of all good things which you did
not fill, and hewn cisterns which you did not dig,
vineyards and olive trees which you did not plant,
and you eat and are satisfied, then watch yourself,
that you do not forget the Lord who brought you
from the land of Egypt, out of the house of slavery.
You shall fear only the Lord your God; and you
shall worship Him and swear by His name. You
shall not follow other gods, any of the gods of the
peoples who surround you, for the Lord your God
in the midst of you is a jealous God; otherwise the
anger of the Lord your God will be kindled against

you, and He will wipe you off the face of the earth.
(Deut. 6:10–15)

Throughout the book of Deuteronomy, Moses
recounts to the Israelites their history since leaving Egypt. He exhorted them to be obedient to the
Lord, listing the prospects of entering a land flowing with milk and honey. He gave instructions and
regulations for life in the land and outlined results
of disobedience. Having given his last instructions
to the people, Moses left them and ascended to
the summit of Pisgah, where the Lord showed him
the whole land across the Jordan, before he died.
(Deut. 34:1–8)

After the death of Moses the Lord appeared to Joshua, instructing
him to cross the Jordan and take the land removing all the inhabitance.
While Israel was in Egypt the people of the land had over 400 years
to repent. They had continued in their idolatry and now their cup of
inequity was full. God plan was for their complete removal, so he could
keep His promise and give the land to Israel. God even went before the
Israelites putting fear in the hearts of those living in the land.

Now it came about after the death of Moses the
servant of the Lord, that the Lord spoke to Joshua
the son of Nun, Moses' servant, saying, "Moses
My servant is dead; now therefore arise, cross this
Jordan, you and all this people, to the land which
I am giving to them, to the sons of Israel. Every
place on which the sole of your foot treads, I have
given it to you, just as I spoke to Moses. From the
wilderness and this Lebanon, even as far as the
great river, the river Euphrates, all the land of the
Hittites, and as far as the Great Sea toward the setting of the sun will be your territory. No man will
be able to stand before you all the days of your life.
Just as I have been with Moses, I will be with you;

I will not fail you or forsake you. Be strong and courageous, for you shall give this people possession of the land, which I swore to their fathers to give them. Only be strong and very courageous; be careful to do according to all the law which Moses My servant commanded you; do not turn from it to the right or to the left, so that you may have success wherever you go. This book of the law shall not depart from your mouth, but you shall meditate on it day and night, so that you may be careful to do according to all that is written in it; for then you will make your way prosperous, and then you will have success. Have I not commanded you? Be strong and courageous! Do not tremble or be dismayed, for the Lord your God is with you wherever you go." (Josh. 1:1–9)

Now it came about when all the kings of the Amorites who were beyond the Jordan to the west, and all the kings of the Canaanites who were by the sea, heard how the Lord had dried up the waters of the Jordan before the sons of Israel until they had crossed, that their hearts melted, and there was no spirit in them any longer because of the sons of Israel. (Josh. 5:1)

Spiritual warfare is universal but concentrated on Israel, God's chosen people as Satan seeks to thwart God's plans. The forces of evil must have been very pleased to have the Israelites enslaved in Egypt for generations. The warfare seems to have become more intense for over forty years as Satan sought to keep Israel out of the Land of Promise and prevent God's promise to Abraham, Isaac, and Jacob from being fulfilled. But Israel's God, who is also the God of Christians, is omnipotent; there is no power in the universe that can prevent His plans from being accomplished. The disobedient generation had perished in the wilderness, and God was now ready to bring the new generation into the Promised Land. Joshua had been commissioned to replace Moses, and God promised to give him success. Joshua then passed on God's promises to the people to assure them of success in taking the land.

> Then Joshua commanded the officers of the people, saying, "Pass through the midst of the camp and command the people, saying, 'Prepare provisions for yourselves, for within three days you are to cross this Jordan, to go in to possess the land which the Lord your God is giving you, to possess it.'" (Josh. 1:10–11)

> Now the Lord said to Joshua, "This day I will begin to exalt you in the sight of all Israel, that they may know that just as I have been with Moses, I will be with you. You shall, moreover, command the priests who are carrying the Ark of the Covenant, saying, 'When you come to the edge of the waters of the Jordan, you shall stand still in the Jordan.'" Then Joshua said to the sons of Israel, "Come here, and hear the words of the Lord your God." Joshua said, "By this you shall know that the living God is among you, and that He will assuredly dispossess from before you the Canaanite, the Hittite, the Hivite, the Perizzite, the Girgashite, the Amorite, and the Jebusite. Behold, the ark of the covenant of the Lord of all the earth is crossing over ahead of you into the Jordan. Now then, take for yourselves twelve men from the tribes of Israel, one man for each tribe. It shall come about when the soles of the feet of the priests who carry the ark of the Lord, the Lord of all the earth, rest in the waters of the Jordan, the waters of the Jordan will be cut off, and the waters which are flowing down from above will stand in one heap." (Josh. 3:7–13)

One of the things man has been slow to learn is that partial obedience only leads to greater problems in the future. This has been the case with Israel throughout their history. They have suffered greatly because of partial obedience or, in many cases, complete disobedience. God had commanded Israel to completely remove the idolatrous people of the land. God had promised Israel success, but early on, Israel failed to give heed and was only partially obedient. The following are cases of partial obedience:

1. Defeat at Ai (Josh. 7)
2. The craftiness of the Gibeonites (Josh. 9)

After these minor failures, the armies of Israel had great success; and the Promised Land was apportioned to each of the tribes (Josh. 13:1–19:51). The tribes who had settled on the east side of the Jordan were allowed to return to their allotments.

> Then Joshua summoned the Reubenites and the Gadites and the half-tribe of Manasseh, and said to them, "You have kept all that Moses the servant of the Lord commanded you, and have listened to my voice in all that I commanded you. You have not forsaken your brothers these many days to this day, but have kept the charge of the commandment of the Lord your God. And now the Lord your God has given rest to your brothers, as He spoke to them; therefore turn now and go to your tents, to the land of your possession, which Moses the servant of the Lord gave you beyond the Jordan. (Josh. 22:1–4)

As Joshua came to the end of his days, he bid Israel farewell, reviewed Israel's history, and exhorted the people to continue in obedience to the Lord (Josh. 23 & 24). With his God-given task complete, the Lord took Joshua.

> It came about after these things that Joshua the son of Nun, the servant of the Lord, died, being one hundred and ten years old. And they buried him in the territory of his inheritance in Timnath-serah,

which is in the hill country of Ephraim, on the
north of Mount Gaash. (Josh. 24:29–30)

After Joshua's passing, the Israelites continued in taking the land;
however, they never completely fulfilled the Lord's command to remove
all the idolatrous peoples from the land. A list of the failures of seven of
the tribes to remove the old inhabitants of the land from their areas is
given in Judges 1:27–35. For their failures, the Israelites were rebuked
by the angel of the Lord.

> Now the angel of the Lord came up from Gilgal
> to Bochim. And he said, "I bought you up out of
> Egypt and led you into the land which I have sworn
> to your fathers; and I said, 'I will never break My
> covenant with you, and as for you, you shall make
> no covenant with the inhabitants of this land;
> you shall tear down their altars.' But you have not
> obeyed Me; what is this you have done? Therefore I
> also said, 'I and their gods will be a snare to you.'"
> When the angel of the Lord spoke these words
> to all the sons of Israel, the people lifted up their
> voices and wept. (Judg. 2:1–4)

Joshua and his generation served the Lord, but after their passing,
a new generation arose that did not know the Lord. The new generation turned from the Lord and began to serve Baal and other gods,
and the demise of Israel started with several events that brought great
hardships.

> All that generation also were gathered to their
> fathers; and there arose another generation after
> them who did not know the Lord, nor yet the
> work which He had done for Israel. Then the sons
> of Israel did evil in the sight of the Lord and served
> the Baals, and they forsook the Lord, the God of
> their fathers, who had brought them out of the land
> of Egypt, and followed other gods from among the
> gods of the peoples who were around them, and

> bowed themselves down to them; thus they pro-
> voked the Lord to anger. So they forsook the Lord
> and served Baal and the Ashtaroth. The anger of
> the Lord burned against Israel, and He gave them
> into the hands of plunderers who plundered them;
> and He sold them into the hands of their enemies
> around them, so that they could no longer stand
> before their enemies. Wherever they went, the hand
> of the Lord was against them for evil, as the Lord
> had spoken and as the Lord had sworn to them, so
> that they were severely distressed. (Judg. 2:10–14)

When the new generation turned from the Lord, the Lord used the nations that had not been removed from the Promised Land to test the obedience of the new generation.

> Now these are the nations, which the Lord left, to
> test Israel by them (that is, all who had not experi-
> enced any of the wars of Canaan; only in order that
> the generations of the sons of Israel might be taught
> war, those who had not experienced it formerly).
> These nations are: the five lords of the Philistines
> and all the Canaanites and the Sidonians and the
> Hivites who lived in Mount Lebanon, from Mount
> Baal-hermon as far as Lebo-hamath. They were for
> testing Israel, to find out if they would obey the
> commandments of the Lord, which He had com-
> manded their fathers through Moses. The sons of
> Israel lived among the Canaanites, the Hittites,
> the Amorites, the Perizzites, the Hivites, and the
> Jebusites; and they took their daughters for them-
> selves as wives, and gave their own daughters to
> their sons, and served their gods. (Judg. 3:1–6)

Because of Israel's disobedience and the Lord's testing, the history of Israel during the time of the judges became a cycle of defeats to the nations, and God raising up judges to deliver Israel when the Israelites cried to Him.

> 1st servitude: Cushan-rishathaim king of Mesopotamia – 8 years. (3:8)
>
> 1st Judge: Othniel son of Kenaz – 40 year deliverance (3:9–11)
>
> 2nd servitude: Eglon the king of Moab - 18 years (3:12–14)
>
> 2nd Judge: Ehud the son of Gera – 80 year deliverance (3:15–26)
>
> 3rd Judge: Shamgar struck 600 Philistines and saved Israel. (3:31)
>
> 3rd servitude: Jabin king of Canaan -20 years (4:1–3)
>
> 4th & 5th Judges: 40 year deliverance (4:4–5:31)
>
> 4th servitude: Midian – 7 years (6:1–6)
>
> 6th Judge: Gideon – 40 year deliverance (6:11–8:28)
>
> Conspiracy of Abimeleck - 3 years (9:1–55)
>
> 7th Judge: Tola of Issachar – 23 years (10:1–2)
>
> 8th judge: Jair the Gileadite – 22 years (10:3)
>
> 4th servitude: Philistines & Ammon – 18 years (10:6–9)
>
> 9th Judge: Jephthat 6 years (11:1–12:7)
>
> 10th Judge: Ibzan of Bethlehem – 7 years (12:8–9)
>
> 11th Judge: Elon the Zebulunite – 10 years (12:11–12)
>
> 12th Judge: Abdon the Pirathonite – 8 years (12:13–14)
>
> 5th servitude: Philistines - 40 years (13:1)
>
> 13th Judge: Samson - 20 years (13:24–16:31)

The remaining day of the judges continued in tumult and upheaval with struggles and warring between the tribes. The people did not call upon God but did their own thing. They seemed to forget that when they called on God, He brought forth a judge to deliver them. Instead of admitting their disobedience, they seemed to blame the cause of their many servitudes to the surrounding nations on the fact that they had no king. Samuel served as the last judge of Israel, and during his day, Israel was severely plagued by the Philistines. At one point, the Philistines even captured the Ark of God. In all of these hardships, Israel continued to ask for a king.

SO YOU WANT A KING

CHAP. 10

Samuel faithfully judged among the people of Israel during all of his days, and the people were content with his judging; however, as Samuel was coming to the end of his days, the elders of the people saw that Samuel's sons did not walk in his ways. And they began again to ask for a king.

> And it came about when Samuel was old that he appointed his sons judges over Israel. Now the name of his firstborn was Joel, and the name of his second, Abijah; they were judging in Beersheba. His sons, however, did not walk in his ways, but turned aside after dishonest gain and took bribes and perverted justice. Then all the elders of Israel gathered together and came to Samuel at Ramah; and they said to him, "Behold, you have grown old, and your sons do not walk in your ways. Now appoint a king for us to judge us like all the nations." (1 Sam. 8:1–5)

Samuel was displeased with the request for a king, but the Lord comforted him by saying that they were not rejecting Samuel but God Himself as they had been doing since He brought them out of Egypt.

> But the thing was displeasing in the sight of Samuel when they said, "Give us a king to judge us." And Samuel prayed to the Lord. The Lord said to Samuel, "Listen to the voice of the people in regard to all that they say to you, for they have not rejected you, but they have rejected Me from being king over them. Like all the deeds, which they have done since the day that I brought them up from Egypt even to this day—in that they have forsaken Me and served other gods—so they are doing to you also. (1 Sam. 8:6–8)

The people asked for a king, and God was ready to give them a king; however, their request was not in accordance with God's will. God's answer in such conditions often brings heartaches. Oh! The people were going to be very pleased with their King at the beginning, but soon, the result was a downhill slide with many troubles. We know the new king was not God's choice for he was a Benjaminite, and God had promised a king forever from the line of Judah. The scepter shall not depart from Judah or the ruler's staff from between his feet " until Shiloh comes, and to him shall be the obedience of the peoples" (Gen. 49:10). Yes, God gave them a king to match their worldly tastes—one who was tall and handsome, one they thought they could be proud of as he led them.

> Now there was a man of Benjamin whose name was Kish the son of Abiel, the son of Zeror, the son of Becorath, the son of Aphiah, the son of a Benjamite, a mighty man of valor. He had a son whose name was Saul, a choice and handsome man, and there was not a more handsome person than he among the sons of Israel; from his shoulders and up he was taller than any of the people. (1 Sam. 9:1–2)

> Now a day before Saul's coming, the Lord had revealed this to Samuel saying, "About this time tomorrow I will send you a man from the land of

Benjamin, and you shall anoint him to be prince over My people Israel; and he will deliver My people from the hand of the Philistines. For I have regarded My people, because their cry has come to Me." When Samuel saw Saul, the Lord said to him, "Behold, the man of whom I spoke to you! This one shall rule over My people." (1 Sam. 9:15–17)

After Samuel had told Saul of God's plans for him, Samuel anointed Saul and presented him to the people.

Then Samuel took the flask of oil, poured it on his head, kissed him and said, "Has not the Lord anointed you a ruler over His inheritance? (1 Sam. 10:1)

Thereafter Samuel called the people together to the Lord at Mizpah; and he said to the sons of Israel, "Thus says the Lord, the God of Israel, 'I brought Israel up from Egypt, and I delivered you from the hand of the Egyptians and from the power of all the kingdoms that were oppressing you.' But you have today rejected your God, who delivers you from all your calamities and your distresses; yet you have said, 'No, but set a king over us!' Now therefore, present yourselves before the Lord by your tribes and by your clans." Thus Samuel brought all the tribes of Israel near, and the tribe of Benjamin was taken by lot. Then he brought the tribe of Benjamin nearby its families, and the Matrite family was taken. And Saul the son of Kish was taken; but when they looked for him, he could not be found. Therefore they inquired further of the Lord, "Has the man come here yet?" So the Lord said, "Behold, he is hiding himself by the baggage." So they ran and took him from there, and when he stood among the people, he was taller than any of the people from his shoulders upward. Samuel said to all the people, "Do you see him whom the Lord has chosen? Surely there is no one like him among all the people." So all the people shouted and said, "Long live the king!" (1 Sam. 10:17–24)

Saul acknowledged his humble beginning and began his rule well. His first victory was over the Ammonites, and he continued delivering Israel from the many nations that plundered Israel.

Saul replied, "Am I not a Benjamite, of the smallest of the tribes of Israel, and my family the least of all the families of the tribe of Benjamin? Why then do you speak to me in this way?" (1 Sam. 9:21)

The next morning Saul put the people in three companies; and they came into the midst of the camp at the morning watch and struck down the Ammonites until the heat of the day. Those who survived were scattered, so that no two of them were left together. (1 Sam. 11:11)

Now when Saul had taken the kingdom over Israel, he fought against all his enemies on every side, against Moab, the sons of Ammon, Edom, the kings of Zobah, and the Philistines; and wherever he turned, he inflicted punishment. He acted valiantly and defeated the Amalekites, and delivered Israel from the hands of those who plundered them. (1 Sam. 14:47–48)

Samuel had told Saul and the people what would happen to them if they turned away from the Lord. But if you still do wickedly, both you and your king will be swept away. (1 Sam. 12:25)

However, with his victories, Saul became more and more self-sufficient and stopped heeding the Lord. Before a battle with the Philistines,

Saul became impatient waiting for Samuel to arrive and offered sacrifices to the Lord. This was not allowed since he was not a priest. When Samuel arrived, he reprimanded Saul and told him that because of his foolish acts, his kingdom would not endure (1 Sam. 13:6–14). On another occasion, when Saul was commanded to go and completely destroy the Amalekites because of their treatment of Israel when Israel came out of Egypt, Saul won the victory but spared Agag, the king, and the best of the flocks and property of the Amelekites.

> Thus says the Lord of hosts, 'I will punish Amalek for what he did to Israel; how he set himself against him on the way while he was coming up from Egypt. Now go and strike Amalek and utterly destroy all that he has, and do not spare him; but put to death both man and woman, child and infant, ox and sheep, camel and donkey.'...Then Samuel said to Saul, "Wait, and let me tell you what the Lord said to me last night." And he said to him, "Speak!" Samuel said, "Is it not true, though you were little in your own eyes, you were made the head of the tribes of Israel? And the Lord anointed you king over Israel, and the Lord sent you on a mission, and said, 'Go and utterly destroy the sinners, the Amalekites, and fight against them until they are exterminated.' Why then did you not obey the voice of the Lord, but rushed upon the spoil and did what was evil in the sight of the Lord?"...But Samuel said to Saul, "I will not return with you; for you have rejected the word of the Lord, and the Lord has rejected you from being king over Israel." As Samuel turned to go, Saul seized the edge of his robe, and it tore. So Samuel said to him, "The Lord has torn the kingdom of Israel from you today and has given it to your neighbor, who is better than you. (1 Sam. 15:2–3, 16–19, 26–28)

Samuel grieved the demise of Saul, but "the Lord regretted that He had made Saul king over Israel" (1 Sam. 15:35b). The Lord asked Samuel to stop grieving for He had business for him to do. Since God had rejected Saul from being king, He was commissioning Samuel to anoint another one to be his replacement.

Now the Lord said to Samuel, "How long will you grieve over Saul, since I have rejected him from being king over Israel? Fill your horn with oil and go; I will send you to Jesse the Bethlehemite, for I have selected a king for Myself among his sons." But Samuel said, "How can I go? When Saul hears of it, he will kill me." And the Lord said, "Take a heifer with you and say, 'I have come to sacrifice to the Lord.' You shall invite Jesse to the sacrifice, and I will show you what you shall do; and you shall anoint for Me the one whom I designate to you." So Samuel did what the Lord said, and came to Bethlehem. And the elders of the city came trembling to meet him and said, "Do you come in peace?" He said, "In peace; I have come to sacrifice to the Lord. Consecrate yourselves and come with me to the sacrifice." He also consecrated Jesse and his sons and invited them to the sacrifice. When they entered, he looked at Eliab and thought, "Surely the Lord's anointed is before Him." But the Lord said to Samuel, "Do not look at his appearance or at the height of his stature, because I have rejected him; for God sees not as man sees, for man looks at the outward appearance, but the Lord looks at the heart." Then Jesse called Abinadab and made him pass before Samuel. And he said, "The Lord has not chosen this one either." Next Jesse made Shammah pass by. And he said, "The Lord has not chosen this one either." Thus Jesse made seven of his sons pass before Samuel. But Samuel said to Jesse, "The Lord has not chosen these." And

Samuel said to Jesse, "Are these all the children?" And he said, "There remains yet the youngest, and behold, he is tending the sheep." Then Samuel said to Jesse, "Send and bring him; for we will not sit down until he comes here." So he sent and brought him in. Now he was ruddy, with beautiful eyes and a handsome appearance. And the Lord said, "Arise, anoint him; for this is he." Then Samuel took the horn of oil and anointed him in the midst of his brothers; and the Spirit of the Lord came mightily upon David from that day forward. And Samuel arose and went to Ramah. (1 Samuel 16:1-13)

From the call and the anointing of David, we can learn several lessons. Saul was chosen largely because of his outward appearance, and his life ended being a disaster. God does not allow bad choices to be repeated. He would not allow Samuel to anoint one of Jesse's more mature sons even though they appeared to have qualities to become a king. David had to be looked for and sought from among the sheep, but God knew his heart. In David, God found a man who would do His will. He was one through whom God could accomplish all His plans, including the redemption of the human race. God's testimony concerning David is recorded for us in the book of Acts of the Apostles 13:22b: "I have found David the son of Jesse, a man after My heart, who will do all My will." The writer of Acts goes on to say, "From the descendants of this man, according to promise, God has brought to Israel a Savior, Jesus." Today we have similar choices: Will we guard our hearts, seek to do God's will—and in so doing, build on something that will be eternal? Or will we be self-sufficient and live for the present?

After Saul was rejected because of his disobedience, the Spirit of the Lord left him and was replaced by an evil spirit. Saul became a pawn of the Evil One and was used by him in an effort to derail God's plan—even to the point of trying to kill God's chosen king.

Now the Spirit of the Lord departed from Saul, and an evil spirit from the Lord terrorized him. Saul's servants then said to him, "Behold now, an evil spirit from God is terrorizing you. (1 Sam. 16:14–15)

Without the Lord's enablement, Saul's life was on a downhill slide; his successes decreased as David's increased. As David's popularity increased, Saul became more jealous; and he spent much of his last days hunting David to kill him.

> It happened as they were coming, when David returned from killing the Philistine, that the women came out of all the cities of Israel, singing and dancing, to meet King Saul, with tambourines, with joy and with musical instruments. The women sang as they played, and said, "Saul has slain his thousands, and David his ten thousands." Then Saul became very angry, for this saying displeased him; and he said, "They have ascribed to David ten thousands, but to me they have ascribed thousands. Now what more can he have but the kingdom?"...Now Saul was afraid of David, for the Lord was with him but had departed from Saul. Therefore Saul removed him from his presence and appointed him as his commander of a thousand; and he went out and came in before the people. David was prospering in all his ways for the Lord was with him. When Saul saw that he was prospering greatly, he dreaded him. But all Israel and Judah loved David, and he went out and came in before them. Then Saul said to David, "Here is my older daughter Merab; I will give her to you as a wife, only be a valiant man for me and fight the Lord's battles." For Saul thought, "My hand shall not be against him, but let the hand of the Philistines be against him." (1 Sam. 18:6–8, 12–17)

Saul became more confused as he sought the Lord but received no answers. Saul's life hit rock bottom when he sought information from the forces of evil—from a medium who was a woman of witchcraft. Saul must have known he was doing wrong, for he disguised himself in going to the witch of En-dor. The Lord was removing Saul from being king, but at this point, His patience was depleted; and He allowed Saul to be killed in battle.

> When Saul inquired of the Lord, the Lord did not answer him, either by dreams or by Urim or by prophets. Then Saul said to his servants, "Seek for me a woman who is a medium, that I may go to her and inquire of her." And his servants said to him, "Behold, there is a woman who is a medium at En-dor." Then Saul disguised himself by putting on other clothes, and went, he and two men with him, and they came to the woman by night; and he said, "Conjure up for me, please, and bring up for me whom I shall name to you." (1 Sam. 28:6–8)

> Now the Philistines were fighting against Israel, and the men of Israel fled from before the Philistines and fell slain on Mount Gilboa. The Philistines overtook Saul and his sons; and the Philistines killed Jonathan and Abinadab and Malchi-shua the sons of Saul. The battle went heavily against Saul, and the archers hit him; and he was badly wounded by the archers. Then Saul said to his armor bearer, "Draw your sword and pierce me through with it, otherwise those uncircumcised will come and pierce me through and make sport of me." But his armor bearer would not, for he was greatly afraid. So Saul took his sword and fell on it. When his armor bearer saw that Saul was dead, he also fell on his sword and died with him. Thus Saul died with his three sons, his armor bearer, and all his men on that day together. (1 Sam. 31:1–6)

After Saul's death, and knowing he had been anointed to be king, David sought direction from the Lord. He was told to go to Hebron, and there He was proclaimed king over Judah.

> David brought up his men who were with him, each with his household; and they lived in the cities of Hebron. Then the men of Judah came, and there anointed David king over the house of Judah. (2 Sam. 2:3–4)

The rest of the nation of Israel, however, did not accept David and rather made Ish-bosheth, Saul's son, king over the remainder of Israel.

> Ish-bosheth, Saul's son, was forty years old when he became king over Israel, and he was king for two years. (2 Sam. 2:10)

The differences in who would be king over the entire nation resulted in civil war in Israel as the forces of evil worked to hinder God's purposes.

> Now there was a long war between the house of Saul and the house of David; and David grew steadily stronger, but the house of Saul grew weaker continually. (2 Sam. 3:1)

With the decline of those following Ish-bosheth, the leaders of Israel came to David to announce they were ready to accept him as king. Finally, the whole nation of Israel was united.

> Then all the tribes of Israel came to David at Hebron and said, "Behold, we are your bone and your flesh. Previously, when Saul was king over us, you were the one who led Israel out and in. And the Lord said to you, 'You will shepherd My people Israel, and you will be a ruler over Israel.'" So all the elders of Israel came to the king at Hebron, and King David made a covenant with them before the Lord at Hebron; then they anointed David king over Israel. David was thirty years old when he became king, and he reigned forty years. (2 Sam. 5:1–4)

After David was installed as king over all Israel, God gave him great victories over his enemies. David captured Zion from the Jebusites (2 Sam. 5:6–7), defeated the Philistines (2 Sam. 5:22–25). Later victories included the Philistines, Moab Zobah, Aram, Ammon, and Amalek (2 Sam. 8:1–14).

> So David reigned over all Israel. And David administered justice and righteousness for all his people. (2 Sam. 8:15)

During the early days of his reign, David realized that he was dwelling in a house of cedar but that the Ark of God was still in the tabernacle (a tent of curtains). It was David's desire to build a temple (house of cedar) for the Ark. God sent a message to David through Nathan, the prophet, that he was a man of war; and He (God) would not have him build a place for Him, but David's son would be allowed to build a "House of God's Name." Although God would not allow David to build Him a house of cedar, God promised to give him a house (descendants) forever.

> Now it came about when the king lived in his house, and the Lord had given him rest on every side from all his enemies, that the king said to Nathan the prophet, "See now, I dwell in a house of cedar, but the ark of God dwells within tent curtains." Nathan said to the king, "Go, do all that is in your mind, for the Lord is with you." But in the same night the word of the Lord came to Nathan, saying, "Go and say to My servant David, 'Thus says the Lord, "Are you the one who should build Me a house to dwell in? For I have not dwelt in a house since the day I brought up the sons of Israel from Egypt, even to this day; but I have been moving about in a tent, even in a tabernacle. Wherever I have gone with all the sons of Israel, did I speak a word with one of the tribes of Israel, which I commanded to shepherd My people Israel, saying,

'Why have you not built Me a house of cedar?'"'
"Now therefore, thus you shall say to My servant David, 'Thus says the Lord of hosts, "I took you from the pasture, from following the sheep, to be ruler over My people Israel. I have been with you wherever you have gone and have cut off all your enemies from before you; and I will make you a great name, like the names of the great men who are on the earth. I will also appoint a place for My people Israel and will plant them, that they may live in their own place and not be disturbed again, nor will the wicked afflict them any more as formerly, even from the day that I commanded judges to be over My people Israel; and I will give you rest from all your enemies. The Lord also declares to you that the Lord will make a house for you. When your days are complete and you lie down with your fathers, I will raise up your descendant after you, who will come forth from you, and I will establish his kingdom. He shall build a house for My name, and I will establish the throne of his kingdom forever. I will be a father to him and he will be a son to Me; when he commits iniquity, I will correct him with the rod of men and the strokes of the sons of men, but My loving kindness shall not depart from him, as I took it away from Saul, whom I removed from before you. Your house and your kingdom shall endure before Me forever; your throne shall be established forever.""'" In accordance with all these words and all this vision, so Nathan spoke to David. (2 Sam. 7:1–17)

"You know that David my father was unable to build a house for the name of the Lord his God because of the wars which surrounded him, until the Lord put them under the soles of his feet. But now the Lord my God has given me rest on every

> side; there is neither adversary nor misfortune. (1 Kings 5:3–4)

> "Nevertheless you shall not build the house, but your son who will be born to you, he will build the house for My name." (1 Kings 8:19)

It has been said that idle hands are the Devil's workshop. This certainly became true in David's life. After many military victories and having his borders secure, David sent his General Joab out to maintain order in his kingdom while he stayed in Jerusalem.

> Then it happened in the spring, at the time when kings go out to battle, that David sent Joab and his servants with him and all Israel, and they destroyed the sons of Ammon and besieged Rabbah. But David stayed at Jerusalem. (2 Sam. 11:1)

With free time, David walked along the roof of the king's house, surveying the outlying regions of Jerusalem. As he was looking, into his view came a beautiful woman. Enquiring whom this woman was, David succumbs to temptation and had her brought to him.

> Now when evening came David arose from his bed and walked around on the roof of the king's house, and from the roof he saw a woman bathing; and the woman was very beautiful in appearance. So David sent and inquired about the woman. And one said, "Is this not Bathsheba, the daughter of Eliam, the wife of Uriah the Hittite?" David sent messengers and took her, and when she came to him, he lay with her; and when she had purified herself from her uncleanness, she returned to her house. (2 Sam. 11:2–4)

David tried to hide his sin, but this became impossible when Bathsheba announced to him that she was pregnant.

> The woman conceived; and she sent and told David, and said, "I am pregnant." (2 Sam. 11:5).

To cover his sin, David instructed General Joab to send Bathsheba's husband, Uriah, into the fiercest battle and then withdraw support so that Uriah would be killed.

> David wrote a letter to Joab and sent it by the hand of Uriah. He had written in the letter, saying, "Place Uriah in the front line of the fiercest battle and withdraw from him, so that he may be struck down and die." (2 Sam. 11:5)

Now we are confronted with the following question: how could God call an adulterer and murderer a friend of God? First, we must realize that there are no degrees of sin with God; sin is sin. We are all undone by sin regardless of how bad we might categorize it. To better understand David's situation, we will contrast his reaction to that of Saul. Both men tried to disregard their sin. In David's case, God made sure David was held accountable and sent the prophet Nathan to him.

> Then the Lord sent Nathan to David. And he came to him and said, "There were two men in one city, the one rich and the other poor. "The rich man had a great many flocks and herds. "But the poor man had nothing except one little ewe lamb which he bought and nourished; and it grew up together with him and his children. It would eat of his bread and drink of his cup and lie in his bosom, and was like a daughter to him. "Now a traveler came to the rich man, and he was unwilling to take from his own flock or his own herd, to prepare for the wayfarer who had come to him; rather he took the poor man's ewe lamb and prepared it for the man who had come to him." (2 Sam. 12:1–4)

David's response to Nathan's story was one of anger (that a person would do such a thing). At that point, Nathan pointed his long, bony finger at David and pronounced, "You are the man."

> Then David's anger burned greatly against the man, and he said to Nathan, "As the Lord lives, surely the man who has done this deserves to die. He must make restitution for the lamb fourfold, because he did this thing and had no compassion." Nathan then said to David, "You are the man!" (2 Sam. 12:5–7)

To us, Saul's disobedience to God's commands may seem small compared to adultery and murder; however, what is of real importance is the reaction of the two men. Saul was sent to wipe out the Amalekites for their treatment of Israel as they came out of Egypt. Saul failed to complete the commands and made lying excuses for his failures.

> Then Samuel said to Saul, "The Lord sent me to anoint you as king over His people, over Israel; now therefore, listen to the words of the Lord. Thus says the Lord of hosts, 'I will punish Amalek for what he did to Israel; how he set himself against him on the way while he was coming up from Egypt. Now go and strike Amalek and utterly destroy all that he has, and do not spare him; but put to death both man and woman, child and infant, ox and sheep, camel and donkey.'" Then Saul summoned the people and numbered them in Telaim, 200,000-foot soldiers and 10,000 men of Judah. Saul came to the city of Amalek and set an ambush in the valley. Saul said to the Kenites, "Go, depart, go down from among the Amalekites, so that I do not destroy you with them; for you showed kindness to all the sons of Israel when they came up from Egypt." So the Kenites departed from among the Amalekites. So Saul defeated the Amalekites, from

> Havilah as you go to Shur, which is east of Egypt. He captured Agag the king of the Amalekites alive, and utterly destroyed all the people with the edge of the sword. But Saul and the people spared Agag and the best of the sheep, the oxen, the fatlings, the lambs, and all that was good, and were not willing to destroy them utterly; but everything despised and worthless, that they utterly destroyed. Then the word of the Lord came to Samuel, saying, "I regret that I have made Saul king, for he has turned back from following Me and has not carried out My commands." (1 Sam. 15:1–11)

We have all heard this one: Saul said, "The people made me do it." Rather than admit his failure and repent, Saul made excuses.

> Then Saul said to Samuel, "I did obey the voice of the Lord, and went on the mission on which the Lord sent me, and have brought back Agag the king of Amalek, and have utterly destroyed the Amalekites. But the people took some of the spoil, sheep and oxen, the choicest of the things devoted to destruction, to sacrifice to the Lord your God at Gilgal." (1 Sam. 15:20–21)

David's reaction to his sin was very different. He did not hide from his sins in spite of their seriousness.

> Then David said to Nathan, "I have sinned against the Lord." And Nathan said to David, "The Lord also has taken away your sin; you shall not die. However, because by this deed you have given occasion to the enemies of the Lord to blaspheme, the child also that is born to you shall surely die." So Nathan went to his house. (2 Sam. 12:13–15)

> Be gracious to me, O God, according to Your loving-kindness; according to the greatness of Your

compassion blot out my transgressions. Wash me thoroughly from my iniquity. And cleanse me from my sin. For I know my transgressions, and my sin is ever before me. Against You, You only, I have sinned, and done what is evil in your sight, so that You are justified when You speak, and blameless when You judge. (Ps. 51:1–4)

David was forgiven, but Nathan told David he had given God's enemies occasion to look down on God.

"The Lord also has taken away your sin; you shall not die. However, because by this deed you have given occasion to the enemies of the Lord to blaspheme. (2 Sam. 12:13b–14a)

Forgiveness often does not wipe out the consequences of sin, and this was the case for David. God used Nathan to tell David that this would be the case in his life.

Why have you despised the word of the Lord by doing evil in His sight? You have struck down Uriah the Hittite with the sword, have taken his wife to be your wife, and have killed him with the sword of the sons of Ammon. Now therefore, the sword shall never depart from your house, because you have despised Me and have taken the wife of Uriah the Hittite to be your wife.' Thus says the Lord, 'Behold, I will raise up evil against you from your own household; I will even take your wives before your eyes and give them to your companion, and he will lie with your wives in broad daylight. Indeed you did it secretly, but I will do this thing before all Israel, and under the sun.'" (2 Sam. 12:9–12)

In David's case, Bathsheba's baby died (2 Sam. 12:15–19), David's son raped David's daughter (2 Sam. 13:1-2, 14), and in revenge a second brother had the rapist killed (2 Sam. 13:28-29). Sounds bad, things got worse. David's son Absalom led a conspiracy against his father in an effort to overtake the kingdom. Many of David's supporters also revolted, and David was forced to flee from Jerusalem (2 Sam. 15:1–14). As David was approaching the end of his days, a second son, Adonijah, attempted to take the kingdom. David suffered greatly from the consequences of his sin, but God also gave him comfort. The Lord gave David a second son by Bathsheba, and he named him Solomon (2 Sam. 12:24). After the conspiracy led by Absalom failed, David was restored as king.

> So the king arose and sat in the gate. When they told all the people, saying, "Behold, the king is sitting in the gate," then all the people came before the king. Now Israel had fled, each to his tent. All the people were quarreling throughout all the tribes of Israel, saying, "The king delivered us from the hand of our enemies and saved us from the hand of the Philistines, but now he has fled out of the land from Absalom. However, Absalom, whom we anointed over us, has died in battle. Now then, why are you silent about bringing the king back?" (2 Sam. 19:8–10)

The Lord had promised David that his son would sit on the throne and build the Lord a house, which David wanted to build. God had made it clear that this would be Solomon; however, the spiritual war had not ended, and Satan tried to put his man on the throne.

> Now Adonijah the son of Haggith exalted himself, saying, "I will be king." So he prepared for himself chariots and horsemen with fifty men to run before him. His father had never crossed him at any time by asking, "Why have you done so?" (1 Kings 1:5–6a)

When Adonijah tried to take the throne by his own initiative quick action by Nathan and Bathsheba brought Solomon to the throne as God had promised.

> Then Nathan spoke to Bathsheba the mother of Solomon, saying, "Have you not heard that Adonijah the son of Haggith has become king, and David our lord does not know it? So now come, please let me give you counsel and save your life and the life of your son Solomon. Go at once to King David and say to him, 'Have you not, my Lord, O king, sworn to your maidservant, saying, "Surely Solomon your son shall be king after me, and he shall sit on my throne." "Why then has Adonijah become king?" (1 Kings 1:11–13)

> Then King David said, "Call to me Zadok the priest, Nathan the prophet, and Benaiah the son of Jehoiada." And they came into the king's presence. The king said to them, "Take with you the servants of your Lord, and have my son Solomon ride on my own mule, and bring him down to Gihon. Let Zadok the priest and Nathan the prophet anoint him there as king over Israel, and blow the trumpet and say, 'Long live King Solomon!' (1 Kings 1:32–34)

> So Zadok the priest, Nathan the prophet, Benaiah the son of Jehoiada, the Cherethites, and the Pelethites went down and had Solomon ride on King David's mule, and brought him to Gihon. Zadok the priest then took the horn of oil from the tent and anointed Solomon. Then they blew the trumpet, and all the people said, "Long live King Solomon!" All the people went up after him, and the people were playing on flutes and rejoicing with great joy, so that the earth shook at their noise. Now

Adonijah and all the guests who were with him heard it as they finished eating. When Joab heard the sound of the trumpet, he said, "Why is the city making such an uproar?" While he was still speaking, behold, Jonathan the son of Abiathar the priest came. Then Adonijah said, "Come in, for you are a valiant man and bring good news." But Jonathan replied to Adonijah, "No! Our lord King David has made Solomon king. The king has also sent with him Zadok the priest, Nathan the prophet, Benaiah the son of Jehoiada, the Cherethites, and the Pelethites; and they have made him ride on the king's mule. Zadok the priest and Nathan the prophet have anointed him king in Gihon, and they have come up from there rejoicing, so that the city is in an uproar. This is the noise, which you have heard. Besides, Solomon has even taken his seat on the throne of the kingdom. Moreover, the king's servants came to bless our Lord King David, saying, 'May your God make the name of Solomon better than your name and his throne greater than your throne!' And the king bowed himself on the bed. The king has also said thus, 'Blessed be the Lord, the God of Israel, who has granted one to sit on my throne today while my own eyes see it.'" (1 Kings 1:38–40, 46–48)

The Lord allowed David to live until Solomon was anointed and know that Solomon had taken his seat on the throne. King David's last official action was to charge his son in how to order the kingdom.

As David's time to die drew near, he charged Solomon his son, saying, I am going the way of all the earth. Be strong, therefore, and show yourself a man. Keep the charge of the Lord your God, to walk in His ways, to keep His statutes, His commandments, His ordinances, and His testimonies, according to what is written in the Law of Moses, that you may succeed in all that you do and wherever you turn, so that the Lord may carry out His promise which He spoke concerning me, saying, 'If your sons are careful of their way, to walk before Me in truth with all their heart and with all their soul, you shall not lack a man on the throne of Israel." (1 Kings2:1–4)

As Solomon begin his reign, God appeared to him, promising to give him his request. In Gibeon the Lord appeared to Solomon in a dream at night; and God said, "Ask what you wish Me to give you" (I Kings 3:5). Solomon's request for a wise and understanding heart so pleased the Lord, that the Lord promised him much beyond his request.

Then Solomon said, "You have shown great loving kindness to Your servant David my father, according as he walked before You in truth and righteousness and uprightness of heart toward You; and You have reserved for him this great loving kindness, that You have given him a son to sit on his throne, as it is this day. Now, O Lord my God, You have made Your servant king in place of my father David, yet I am but a little child; I do not know how to go out or come in. Your servant is in the midst of Your people, which You have chosen, a great people who are too many to be numbered or counted. So give Your servant an understanding heart to judge Your people to discern between good and evil. For who is able to judge this great people of Yours?" It was pleasing in the sight of the Lord that Solomon had asked this thing. God said to him, "Because you have asked this thing and have not asked for yourself long life, nor have asked riches for yourself, nor have you asked for the life of your enemies, but have asked for yourself discernment to understand justice, behold, I have done according to your words. Behold, I have given you a wise and discerning heart, so that there has been no one like you before you, nor shall one like you arise after you. I have also given you what you have not asked, both riches and honor, so that there will not be any among the kings like you all your days. If you walk in My ways, keeping My statutes and commandments, as your father David walked, then I will prolong your days." (1 Kings 3:6–14)

Solomon's reign had a very successful beginning as God gave him all that He had promised. Solomon extended the borders of his kingdom, his wisdom was known by many, both he and Israel became wealthy and affluent, and he was able to build the temple, just like God had told his father David.

Now Solomon ruled over all the kingdoms from the River to the land of the Philistines and to the border of Egypt; they brought tribute and served Solomon all the days of his life. (1 Kings 4:21)

Now God gave Solomon wisdom and very great discernment and breadth of mind, like the sand that is on the seashore. Solomon's wisdom surpassed the wisdom of all the sons of the east and all the wisdom of Egypt. For he was wiser than all men, than Ethan the Ezrahite, Heman, Calcol and Darda, the sons of Mahol; and his fame was known in all the surrounding nations. He also spoke 3,000 proverbs, and his songs were 1,005. He spoke of trees, from the cedar that is in Lebanon even to the hyssop that grows on the wall; he spoke also of animals and birds and creeping things and fish. Men came from all peoples to hear the wisdom of Solomon, from all the kings of the earth who had heard of his wisdom. (1 Kings 4:29–34)

> Now it came about in the four hundred and eight-
> ieth year after the sons of Israel came out of the
> land of Egypt, in the fourth year of Solomon's reign
> over Israel, in the month of Ziv which is the sec-
> ond month, that he began to build the house of the
> Lord. (1 Kings 6:1)

> So Solomon built the house and finished it. In the
> fourth year the foundation of the house of the Lord
> was laid, in the month of Ziv. In the eleventh year,
> in the month of Bul, which is the eighth month,
> the house was finished throughout all its parts and
> according to all its plans. So he was seven years in
> building it. (1 Kings 6:14, 37–38)

A great start is never sufficient if one does not finish well. So
was the case with Solomon; how could one given such wisdom fall so
far? Well it seems Solomon like his father had a woman problem, but
his problem far exceeded that of his father David. Yes, Solomon was
human, and he succumbed to the flesh.

> Now King Solomon loved many foreign women
> along with the daughter of Pharaoh: Moabite,
> Ammonite, Edomite, Sidonian, and Hittite
> women, from the nations concerning which the
> Lord had said to the sons of Israel, "You shall not
> associate with them, nor shall they associate with
> you, for they will surely turn your heart away after
> their gods." Solomon held fast to these in love. He
> had seven hundred wives, princesses, and three
> hundred concubines, and his wives turned his
> heart away. For when Solomon was old, his wives
> turned his heart away after other gods; and his
> heart was not wholly devoted to the Lord his God,
> as the heart of David his father had been. (1 Kings
> 11:1–4)

It seems impossible that a person given so much wisdom could fall so far, but it happened to Solomon, and should cause each of us to keep our eyes on the Lord and continually seek His will. Not only did Solomon lose much including his close relationship with God, his actions would result in the division of the nation of Israel, which caused extreme hardship for his people.

> Now the Lord was angry with Solomon because his heart was turned away from the Lord, the God of Israel, who had appeared to him twice, and had commanded him concerning this thing, that he should not go after other gods; but he did not observe what the Lord had commanded. So the Lord said to Solomon, "Because you have done this, and you have not kept My covenant and My statutes, which I have commanded you, I will surely tear the kingdom from you, and will give it to your servant. Nevertheless I will not do it in your days for the sake of your father David, but I will tear it out of the hand of your son. However, I will not tear away all the kingdom, but I will give one tribe to your son for the sake of My servant David and for the sake of Jerusalem which I have chosen." (1 Kings 11:9–13)

Solomon turned from the Lord in disobedience, and in so doing moved himself and his nation out from under God's umbrella of protection. Enemies penetrated Israel's once secure borders, and within the nation of Israel there was rebellion against King Solomon.

> Then the Lord raised up an adversary to Solomon, Hadad the Edomite; he was of the royal line in Edom. (1 Kings 11:9–14)

> God also raised up another adversary to him, Rezon the son of Eliada, (1 Kings 11:23)

> Then Jeroboam the son of Nebat, an Ephraimite of
> Zeredah, Solomon's servant, whose mother's name
> was Zeruah, a widow, also rebelled against the king.
> (1 Kings 11:26)

God's displeasure with Solomon was so great, that He was going to allow the division of Israel as a nation. God would use Jeroboam rebellion to accomplish this.

> Now this was the reason why he rebelled against
> the king: Solomon built the Millo, and closed up
> the breach of the city of his father David. Now the
> man Jeroboam was a valiant warrior, and when
> Solomon saw that the young man was industrious,
> he appointed him over all the forced labor of the
> house of Joseph. It came about at that time, when
> Jeroboam went out of Jerusalem, that the prophet
> Ahijah the Shilonite found him on the road. Now
> Ahijah had clothed himself with a new cloak; and
> both of them were alone in the field. Then Ahijah
> took hold of the new cloak, which was on him and
> tore it into twelve pieces. He said to Jeroboam,
> "Take for yourself ten pieces; for thus says the
> Lord, the God of Israel, 'Behold, I will tear the
> kingdom out of the hand of Solomon and give you
> ten tribes but he will have one tribe, for the sake of
> My servant David and for the sake of Jerusalem,
> the city which I have chosen from all the tribes of
> Israel, because they have forsaken Me, and have
> worshiped Ashtoreth the goddess of the Sidonians,
> Chemosh the god of Moab, and Milcom the god
> of the sons of Ammon; and they have not walked
> in My ways, doing what is right in My sight and
> observing My statutes and My ordinances, as his
> father David did. Nevertheless I will not take the
> whole kingdom out of his hand, but I will make
> him ruler all the days of his life, for the sake of My

servant David whom I chose, who observed My commandments and My statutes; but I will take the kingdom from his son's hand and give it to you, even ten tribes. But to his son I will give one tribe, that My servant David may have a lamp always before Me in Jerusalem, the city where I have chosen for Myself to put My name. I will take you, and you shall reign over whatever you desire, and you shall be king over Israel. Then it will be, that if you listen to all that I command you and walk in My ways, and do what is right in My sight by observing My statutes and My commandments, as My servant David did, then I will be with you and build you an enduring house as I built for David, and I will give Israel to you. Thus I will afflict the descendants of David for this, but not always.'" Solomon sought therefore to put Jeroboam to death; but Jeroboam arose and fled to Egypt to Shishak king of Egypt, and he was in Egypt until the death of Solomon. (1 Kings 11:27–40)

David prepared and equipped Solomon to replace himself as king. There is little evidence that Solomon did the same for his son. At Solomon's death Rehoboam came to the throne ill prepared to lead Israel. Rehoboam was also a poor judge of character, which resulted in him surrounding himself with poor counselors.

And Solomon slept with his fathers and was buried in the city of his father David, and his son Rehoboam reigned in his place. Then Rehoboam went to Shechem, for all Israel had come to Shechem to make him king. Now when Jeroboam the son of Nebat heard of it, he was living in Egypt (for he was yet in Egypt, where he had fled from the presence of King Solomon). Then they sent and called him, and Jeroboam and all the assembly of Israel came and spoke to Rehoboam, saying, "Your father made our yoke hard; now therefore lighten the hard service of your father and his heavy yoke which he put on us, and we will serve you." Then he said to them, "Depart for three days, then return to me." So the people departed. King Rehoboam consulted with the elders who had served his father Solomon while he was still alive, saying, "How do you counsel me to answer this people?" Then they spoke to him, saying, "If you will be a servant to this people today, and will serve them and grant them their petition, and speak good words to them, then they will be your servants forever." But he forsook the counsel of the elders, which they had given him, and consulted with the young men who grew up with him and served him. So he said to them, "What counsel do you give that we may answer this people who have spoken to me, saying, 'Lighten the yoke which your father put on us'?" The young men who grew up with him spoke to him, saying, "Thus you shall say to this people who spoke to you, saying, 'Your father made our yoke heavy, now you make it lighter for us!' But you shall speak to them, 'My little finger is thicker than my father's loins! Whereas my father loaded you with a heavy yoke, I will add to your yoke; my father disciplined you with whips, but I will discipline you with scorpions.'" (1 Kings 11:43–12:11)

Rehoboam listened to his fellows and spoke harshly to the people on their return to hear his decision. The result was the people rebelled and later turned to Jeroboam as the Lord had foretold through the prophet Ahijah.

When all Israel saw that the king did not listen to them, the people answered the king, saying, "What portion do we have in David? We have no inheritance in the son of Jesse; To your tents, O Israel!

> Now look after your own house, David!" So Israel
> departed to their tents. But as for the sons of Israel
> who lived in the cities of Judah, Rehoboam reigned
> over them. Then King Rehoboam sent Adoram,
> who was over the forced labor, and all Israel stoned
> him to death. And King Rehoboam made haste to
> mount his chariot to flee to Jerusalem. So Israel
> has been in rebellion against the house of David to
> this day. It came about when all Israel heard that
> Jeroboam had returned, that they sent and called
> him to the assembly and made him king over all
> Israel. None but the tribe of Judah followed the
> house of David. (1 Kings 12:16–20)

Jeroboam was quick to forget God's promises to be with him if he followed God's statutes and commandments. Instead he did all he could to keep them from going up to Jerusalem to worship and return to following Rehoboam. In order to prevent the people from going to Jerusalem to worship, he set up points for false worship with golden calves.

> Then Jeroboam built Shechem in the hill coun-
> try of Ephraim, and lived there. And he went out
> from there and built Penuel. Jeroboam said in
> his heart, "Now the kingdom will return to the
> house of David. If this people go up to offer sac-
> rifices in the house of the Lord at Jerusalem, then
> the heart of this people will return to their lord,
> even to Rehoboam king of Judah; and they will kill
> me and return to Rehoboam king of Judah." So
> the king consulted, and made two golden calves,
> and he said to them, "It is too much for you to go
> up to Jerusalem; behold your gods, O Israel, that
> brought you up from the land of Egypt." (1 Kings
> 12:25–28)

Because of Jeroboam's disobedience, not only did the Lord remove Jeroboam from being king, but also said his whole house would be cut off. Moreover, the Lord will raise up for Himself a king over Israel who will cut off the house of Jeroboam this day and from now on (1 Kings14:14). Jeroboam became a byword for most of those who followed him. "For he walked in all the way of Jeroboam the son of Nebat and in his sins which he made Israel sin." During its entire history, the Northern Kingdom, Israel, never had a good king. Sadly the people followed the ways of their evil kings. Because of her disobedience, the Lord allowed Israel to be afflicted by neighboring nations. Early affliction came from the Arameans, later the Assyrians required tribute from Israel. The evils throughout the land of Israel, eventually brought God's long suffering to an end. Israel's last king Hoshea conspired against Assyria in order to stop paying the tribute due. God used this to bring Shalmanezer V (727–722 BC), King of Assyria, against Israel in final punishment. Shalmaneser king of Assyria came up against Samaria and besieged it (2 Kings 18:9b). Shalmaneser besieged Israel's capital city, Samaria, for three years and finally captured it. After capturing Samaria in 722 BC, Assyria carried the Israelites into captivity. This ended the existence of Israel after 200 years, which had begun with the reign of Jeroboam I in 922 BC.

> Hoshea the son of Elah became king over Israel in Samaria, and reigned nine years. He did evil in the sight of the Lord, only not as the kings of Israel who were before him. Shalmaneser king of Assyria came up against him, and Hoshea became his servant and paid him tribute. But the king of Assyria found conspiracy in Hoshea, who had sent messengers to So king of Egypt and had offered no tribute to the king of Assyria, as he had done year by year; so the king of Assyria shut him up and bound him in prison. Then the king of Assyria invaded the whole land and went up to Samaria and besieged it three years. In the ninth year of Hoshea, the king of Assyria captured Samaria and carried Israel away into exile to Assyria. (2 Kings17:1b–6a)

Why did God allow Israel to fall?

> Now this came about because the sons of Israel
> had sinned against the Lord their God, who had
> brought them up from the land of Egypt from
> under the hand of Pharaoh, king of Egypt, and
> they had feared other gods and walked in the cus-
> toms of the nations whom the Lord had driven out
> before the sons of Israel, and in the customs of the
> kings of Israel which they had introduced. The sons
> of Israel did things secretly, which were not right
> against the Lord their God. Moreover, they built
> for themselves high places in all their towns, from
> watchtower to fortified city. They set for them-
> selves sacred pillars and Asherim on every high hill
> and under every green tree, and there they burned
> incense on all the high places as the nations did
> which the Lord had carried away to exile before
> them; and they did evil things provoking the Lord.
> They served idols, concerning which the Lord had
> said to them, "You shall not do this thing." Yet
> the Lord warned Israel and Judah through all His
> prophets and every seer, saying, "Turn from your
> evil ways and keep My commandments, My stat-
> utes according to all the law which I commanded
> your fathers, and which I sent to you through My
> servants the prophets." However, they did not
> listen, but stiffened their neck like their fathers,
> who did not believe in the Lord their God. They
> rejected His statutes and His covenant, which He
> made with their fathers and His warnings with
> which He warned them. And they followed vanity
> and became vain, and went after the nations, which
> surrounded them, concerning which the Lord had
> commanded them not to do like them. They for-
> sook all the commandments of the Lord their God
> and made for themselves molten images, even two

calves, and made an Asherah and worshiped all the host of heaven and served Baal. Then they made their sons and their daughters pass through the fire, and practiced divination and enchantments, and sold themselves to do evil in the sight of the Lord, provoking Him. So the Lord was very angry with Israel and removed them from His sight; none was left except the tribe of Judah. (2 Kings 17:7–18)

During this time Judah in the south, had a more checkered history; having both good and bad kings. Assyria also attacked Judah, but God gave them protection. An example of God's protection of Judah was during the days when Hezekiah was King. Sennacherib (705–681 BC), who was then king of Assyria, came against Judah, besieged its cities, and threatened Jerusalem. King Hezekiah humbled himself and sent to the prophet Isaiah for advice. Isaiah's answer was thus you shall say to your master, 'Thus says the Lord,

"Do not be afraid because of the words that you have heard, with which the servants of the king of Assyria have blasphemed Me. Behold, I will put a spirit in him so that he will hear a rumor and return to his own land. And I will make him fall by the sword in his own land.'" (2 Kings 19:6–7)

After this Sennacherib sent another threat to Hezekiah.

"Do not let your God in whom you trust deceive you saying, 'Jerusalem will not be given into the hand of the king of Assyria. Behold, you have heard what the kings of Assyria have done to all the lands, destroying them completely. So will you be spared? Did the gods of those nations, which my fathers destroyed, deliver them, even Gozan and Haran and Rezeph and the sons of Eden who were in

Telassar? Where is the king of Hamath, the king of Arpad, the king of the city of Sepharvaim, and of Hena and Ivvah?'" (2 Kings 19:10–13)

After reading the threatened letter, Hezekiah went up to the temple, laid the letter out before the Lord and prayed.

> "O Lord, the God of Israel, who are enthroned above the cherubim, You are the God, You alone, of all the kingdoms of the earth. You have made heaven and earth. Incline Your ear, O Lord, and hear; open Your eyes, O Lord, and see; and listen to the words of Sennacherib, which he has sent to reproach the living God. Truly, O Lord, the kings of Assyria have devastated the nations and their lands and have cast their gods into the fire, for they were not gods but the work of men's hands, wood and stone. So they have destroyed them. Now, O Lord our God, I pray, deliver us from his hand that all the kingdoms of the earth may know that You alone, O Lord, are God." (2 Kings 19:15–19)

And the Lord sent Hezekiah a message by the prophet Isaiah.

> Therefore thus says the Lord concerning the king of Assyria, "He will not come to this city or shoot an arrow there; and he will not come before it with a shield or throw up a siege ramp against it. By the way that he came, by the same he will return, and he shall not come to this city,'" declares the Lord. 'For I will defend this city to save it for My own sake and for My servant David's sake.'" (2 Kings 19:32–34)

The result that followed is proof that it is not wise to mock the Lord, and to do so only brings disaster to the mocker.

> Then it happened that night that the angel of the
> Lord went out and struck 185,000 in the camp
> of the Assyrians; and when men rose early in
> the morning, behold, all of them were dead. So
> Sennacherib king of Assyria departed and returned
> home, and lived at Nineveh. It came about as he
> was worshiping in the house of Nisroch his god,
> that Adrammelech and Sharezer killed him with
> the sword; and they escaped into the land of Ararat.
> And Esarhaddon his son became king in his place.
> (2 Kings 19:35–37)

Another example from the kings of Judah, who walked with God,
is Josiah.

> He did right in the sight of the Lord and walked
> in all the way of his father David, nor did he turn
> aside to the right or to the left. (2 Kings 22:2)

During his reign Josiah called for repairs to be made to the temple. It was during this time of temple repair, that "The Book of the
Law" was discovered, which had lain unheeded for years in the deteri-
orating temple.

> Then Hilkiah the high priest said to Shaphan the
> scribe, "I have found the book of the law in the
> house of the Lord." And Hilkiah gave the book to
> Shaphan who read it. Shaphan the scribe came to
> the king and brought back word to the king and
> said, "Your servants have emptied out the money
> that was found in the house, and have delivered it
> into the hand of the workmen who have the over-
> sight of the house of the Lord." Moreover, Shaphan
> the scribe told the king saying, "Hilkiah the priest
> has given me a book." And Shaphan read it in the
> presence of the king. When the king heard the
> words of the book of the law, he tore his clothes.
> Then the king commanded Hilkiah the priest,

Ahikam the son of Shaphan, Achbor the son of Micaiah, Shaphan the scribe, and Asaiah the king's servant saying, "Go, inquire of the Lord for me and the people and all Judah concerning the words of this book that has been found, for great is the wrath of the Lord that burns against us, because our fathers have not listened to the words of this book, to do according to all that is written concerning us." (2 Kings 22:8–13)

Josiah and his court were quick to realize the dangers facing them and all of Judah because of the neglect of God's Word, and sent to the prophetess Huldah to inquire of the Lord about what they faced. Unfortunately God's patience with disobedience only lasts so long. The prophetess' message was one of coming judgment.

She said to them, "Thus says the Lord God of Israel, 'Tell the man who sent you to me, thus says the Lord, "Behold, I bring evil on this place and on its Inhabitants, even all the words of the book, which the king of Judah has read. Because they have forsaken Me and have burned incense to other gods that they might provoke Me to anger with all the work of their hands, therefore My wrath burns against this place, and it shall not be quenched."' But to the king of Judah who sent you to inquire of the Lord thus shall you say to him, 'Thus says the Lord God of Israel, "Regarding the words which you have heard, because your heart was tender and you humbled yourself before the Lord when you heard what I spoke against this place and against its inhabitants that they should become a desolation and a curse, and you have torn your clothes and wept before Me, I truly have heard you," declares the Lord. "Therefore, behold, I will gather you to your fathers, and you will be gathered to your grave in peace, and your eyes will not see all the evil

> which I will bring on this place."'"'" So they brought
> back word to the king. (2 Kings 22:15–20)

Josiah covenanted to walk with the Lord, removed idolatrous practices from the land, and reinstituted the Passover. It is said of Josiah:

> Before him there was no king like him who turned
> to the Lord with all his heart and with all his soul
> and with all his might, according to all the Law
> of Moses; nor did any like him arise after him (2
> Kings 23:25).

In spite of the efforts of Josiah the only consolation he received
was the words of the prophetess that the Lord's judgment would not
fall in his day, but judgment was announced as certain.

> However, the Lord did not turn from the fierceness
> of His great wrath with which His anger burned
> against Judah, because of all the provocations with
> which Manasseh had provoked Him. The Lord
> said, "I will remove Judah also from My sight, as I
> have removed Israel. And I will cast off Jerusalem,
> this city which I have chosen, and the temple of
> which I said, 'My name shall be there.'" (2 Kings
> 23:26–27)

The reforms of Josiah are often spoken of as a revival, but we can
question: was there revival? Josiah's three sons and one grandson all
who succeeded him were evil. The Bible says of them: "They did evil
in the sight of the Lord, according to all that their fathers had done."
Scripture says of Jehoiachin/Coniah, the grandson of Josiah that he
would be childless.

> "As I live," declares the Lord, "even though Coniah
> the son of Jehoiakim king of Judah were a signet
> ring on My right hand, yet I would pull you off;
> and I will give you over into the hand of those
> who are seeking your life, yes, into the hand of

those whom you dread, even into the hand of Nebuchadnezzar king of Babylon and into the hand of the Chaldeans. I will hurl you and your mother who bore you into another country where you were not born, and there you will die. But as for the land to which they desire to return, they will not return to it. "Is this man Coniah a despised, shattered jar? Or is he an undesirable vessel? Why have he and his descendants been hurled out and cast into a land that they had not known? O land, land, land. Hear the word of the Lord! "Thus says the Lord, 'Write this man down childless, a man who will not prosper in his days; For no man of his descendants will prosper sitting on the throne of David or ruling again in Judah.'" (Jer. 22:24–30)

Disobedience causes problems, and we are left with three problems: (1) There was no fruit in Josiah's family from his revival; (2) Josiah's grandson was pronounced as being childless; (3) Judah was told they would go into captivity under Nebuchadnezzar. Spiritual warfare was raging and Satan must have been smiling. He could see no results from Josiah's reform. He seeming had brought an end to the Messianic line. Jehioiachin would be childless and was promised that none of his descendants would prosper sitting on the throne of David. Abraham had been promised a land forever for his descendants (Gen. 12:7), and now Judah was following Israel into captivity.

Things may have been looking gloomy, but our God is the God of the impossible (Luke 1:37). Will there be fruit from Josiah's revival, only time will tell. What about the line of Messiah? God must have a future surprise for us. How will God be able to keep His promise to Abraham of a land forever?

THE COST OF DISOBEDIENCE   CHAP. 11

God had told Josiah, through the prophetess Huldah, that Judah would become a desolation. This happened in the days of Nebuchadnezzar of Babylon. In three campaigns he left Judah and Jerusalem a wasteland. In 605 BC, after a decisive victory over Egypt, Nebuchadnezzar turned his conquest efforts on Jerusalem. His efforts included the deportation of captives, among these was Daniel. Nebuchadnezzar return to besiege Jerusalem and took possession of it in 597 BC. He gathered a group of 1000 captives (2 Kings 24:14), which included King Jehoiachin, and Ezekiel the prophet. Nebuchadnezzar set up Zedikiah as his puppet king in Jerusalem. Zedekiah ruled until he rebelled against Nebuchadnezzar (2 Kings 24:20). Zedikiah's rebellion resulted in Nebuchadnezzar's armies returning to besiege Jerusalem the third time, which resulted in the complete destruction of Jerusalem, and making Judah largely a wasteland.

> Now on the seventh day of the fifth month, which was the nineteenth year of King Nebuchadnezzar, king of Babylon, Nebuzaradan the captain of the guard, a servant of the king of Babylon came to Jerusalem. He burned the house of the Lord, the king's house, and all the houses of Jerusalem; even

every great house he burned with fire. So all the army of the Chaldeans who were with the captain of the guard broke down the walls around Jerusalem. Then the rest of the people who were left in the city and the deserters with the captain of the guard broke down the walls around Jerusalem. Then the rest of the people who were left in the city and the deserters who had deserted who had deserted to the king of Babylon and the rest of the people, Nebuzaradan the captain of the guard carried away into exile. But the captain of the guard left some of the poorest of the land to be vinedressers and plowmen. (2 Kings 25:8–12)

The disobedience of the people of Judah had definitely left the entire land in destruction. These were dark days. God's chosen people had been left in disarray; however, even though God severely judges sin, He will not allow His plans to be thwarted. To find hope in this situation we must go back to 605 BC and Nebuchadnezzar's first deportation from Judah. Included in this deportation were the prophet Daniel and his three friends (Dan. 1:6–7). It was Nebuchadnezzar's practice as he captured different people to train certain promised young men from these people to represent him in his rule over these various people. To represent him among the people of Judah, Daniel and his three friends had been chosen. At the time of the final destruction of Jerusalem, Daniel had graduated Magna cum laude from the University of Babylon and had been in training and service to Nebuchadnezzar for nineteen years. He was now a young man in his thirties.

To better understand Daniel's situation lets go back to his first days in Babylon. The young captives that Nebuchadnezzar had in training were offered the same diet as the king. The king appointed for them a daily ration from the king's choice food and from the wine which he drank (Dan. 1:5a). When this choice diet was set before Daniel and his three friends, Daniel asked for a different diet.

But Daniel made up his mind that he would not defile himself with the king's choice food or with the wine which he drank; so he sought permission from the commander of the officials that he might not defile himself. Now God granted Daniel favor and compassion in the sight of the commander of the officials, and the commander of the officials said to Daniel, "I am afraid of my lord the king, who has appointed your food and your drink; for why should he see your faces looking more haggard than the youths who are your own age? Then you would make me forfeit my head to the king." But Daniel said to the overseer whom the commander of the officials had appointed over Daniel, Hananiah, Mishael and Azariah, "Please test your servants for ten days, and let us be given some vegetables to eat and water to drink. Then let our appearance be observed in your presence and the appearance of the youths who are eating the king's choice food; and deal with your servants according to what you see." So he listened to them in this matter and tested them for ten days. At the end of ten days their appearance seemed better and they were fatter than all the youths who had been eating the king's choice food. So the overseer continued to withhold their choice food and the wine they were to drink, and kept giving them vegetables. (Dan. 1:8–16)

Why would Daniel ask for a diet of vegetables and turn down the meats for the king's table? Scripture tells us he did not want to be defiled. Daniel knew the dietary laws of his people, in all likelihood the food from the king's table was not kosher, and Daniel put God before the king. Where did Daniel get such knowledge? The Law of Moses was a closed book, lost in the temple ruins before the days of Josiah. Could Daniel have been there when Josiah read the Law to his people (2 Kings 23:1–2)? Daniel would have been a teenager at the time. He could have heard Josiah's reading, for scripture says all the people were there from the youngest to the oldest. Yes, there undoubtedly was fruit from Josiah's revival. Josiah's own sons did not follow their father's walk with the Lord, but God has always had His person to carry out His plan. Daniel and his three friends appear to be fruit from Josiah's reform, prepared to do God's bidding. When tested before Nebuchadnezzar the four passed with flying colors and entered the king's service.

> As for these four youths, God gave them knowledge and intelligence in every branch of literature and wisdom; Daniel even understood all kinds of visions and dreams. Then at the end of the days, which the king had specified for presenting them, the commander of the officials presented them before Nebuchadnezzar. The king talked with them, and out of them all not one was found like Daniel, Hananiah, Mishael and Azariah; so they entered the king's personal service. As for every matter of wisdom and understanding about which the king consulted them, he found them ten times better than all the magicians and conjurers who were in all his realm. (Dan. 1:17–20)

Later after Daniel interpreted Nebuchadnezzar's first dream, Daniel was elevated again, and granted authority over the province of Babylon, as he served in the King's court. At this time, at Daniel's request his three friends were also elevated and given administrative power over the province of Babylon.

> Then the king promoted Daniel and gave him many great gifts, and he made him ruler over the whole province of Babylon and chief prefect over all the wise men of Babylon. And Daniel made request of the king, and he appointed Shadrach, Meshach and Abed-nego over the administration of the province of Babylon, while Daniel was at the king's court. (Dan. 2:48–49)

God certainly used these four to preserve His people during the time of captivity. God does use severe means to correct the disobedience of His people; however, He does protect them at the same time. He will never forget the promises He has made to the patriarchs, as well as promises to all His people. The fruit of Daniel's life goes far beyond those he helped protect during his life. As a prophet, God used Daniel to write a book that has encouraged and strengthened people throughout history to stand for the Lord. In Daniel's book God has revealed a portion of His plan of the ages, reached into eternity future. Even in the dark days we live in, the Book of Daniel comforts and encourages us; and will continue to do so for those living in the difficult times of the future. Was there fruit from Josiah's revival? Daniel's life says *definitely*.

DANIEL'S ORDER OF EMPIRES

Scripture speaks of a "Time of the Gentiles" (Ezek. 30:3 & Luke 21:24). This is a time when Israel will not have a king, nor will Israel be a prominent world power. This time begin when the forces of Nebuchadnezzar carried the last king of Judah into captivity, leaving Judah in ruins and without a king. The "times of the Gentiles" will continue until Israel once again has a King. We believe that King will be none other than the King of King, the Lord Jesus Christ. The predominant world powers during this time are revealed in two scriptural passages. First in Daniel chapter 2 where Daniel gives the interpretation of Nebuchadnezzar's dream. And secondly in chapter 7 an angel gives the interpretation of Daniel's dream. The two visions speak of the same time periods. In chapter 2, Nebuchadnezzar vision is of a magnificent statue. This vision gives us the human view of the great empires of history. Man sees history as a picture of man's accomplishments. In chapter 7 we see God's view of the empires of history, beastly forces where humans were used and abused. The great architectural accomplishments built on the backs of slaves. Men and women degraded at the expense of those in power.

Chapter 2	Gold	Silver	Bronze	Iron/clay	Stone w/o hands
Chapter 7	Lion	Bear	Leopard	Composite beast	Ancient of Days
	Babylon	Persia	Greece	Rome	Christ's Kingdom
BC	605–539	539–331	331–168	168–?	?–forever

According to the visions of Daniel only four empires precede Christ's kingdom. One must ask how can this be, the Roman Empire is long past. The first three empires of the vision in Daniel, Babylon, Persia and Greece were defeated in battle. This was not the case with Roman. As different Romans struggled to be Caesar, legions fought other legions in the support of the individual of their choice. In the process, the strength of Rome was decimated, barbarian hordes swept in, and the empire fell apart; however, there has always been a semblance of Rome though out the area that was once the Roman Empire. Through the ages of recent history many have attempted to reassemble the empire, such men as Charlemagne, Napoleon, Otto von Bismarck, Hitler, and Mussolini. These men all failed; however, Bible prophecy foretells of the rise of one who for a short time will restore the empire, just prior to the second advent of Christ to establish his everlasting kingdom. It has been said, "Save your confederate money. The south will rise again." That is very uncertain. It may be wiser to say, "Save your Euros. Rome will rise again!"

DANIEL'S SEVENTY WEEKS (DAN. 9:24–27)

Daniel was a student of the scriptures and particularly of the Prophecy of Jeremiah. Jeremiah had foretold that the captivity would last seventy years. When Israel was established as a nation, God had commanded them that every seventh year was to be a Sabbath year, when the land was to lay at rest. In their greed the Israelite had failed to observe seventy Sabbath years. Sending Judah into captivity God would reclaim the Sabbath years that were not observed, and the land would lie at rest seventy years.

> "Therefore thus says the Lord of hosts, 'Because you have not obeyed My words, behold, I will send and take all the families of the north,' declares the Lord, 'and I will send to Nebuchadnezzar king of Babylon, My servant, and will bring them against this land and against its inhabitants and against all these nations round about; and I will utterly destroy them and make them a horror and a hissing, and an everlasting desolation. Moreover, I will take from them the voice of joy and the voice of gladness, the voice of the bridegroom and the voice of the bride, the sound of the millstones and the light of the lamp. This whole land will be desolation and a horror, and these nations will serve the king of Babylon seventy years. 'Then it will be when seventy years are completed I will punish the king of Babylon and that nation,' declares the Lord, 'for their iniquity, and the land of the Chaldeans; and I will make it an everlasting desolation. I will bring upon that land all My words, which I have pronounced, against it, all that is written in this book, which Jeremiah has prophesied against all the nations. (Jer. 25:8–13)

> "For thus says the Lord, 'When seventy years have been completed for Babylon, I will visit you and fulfill My good word to you, to bring you back to this place. For I know the plans that I have for you,' declares the Lord, 'plans for welfare and not for calamity to give you a future and a hope. Then you will call upon Me and come and pray to Me, and I will listen to you. You will seek Me and find Me when you search for Me with all your heart. I will be found by you,' declares the Lord, 'and I will

> restore your fortunes and will gather you from all
> the nations and from all the places where I have
> driven you,' declares the Lord, 'and I will bring you
> back to the place from where I sent you into exile.
> (Jer. 29:10–14)

Daniel was now an old man; it had been nearly seventy years since he had been carried into captivity. In Daniel chapter 9, Daniel is praying, asking the Lord how long until the captivity ends. It seems that Daniel may have thought when the captivity was over, the Israelites would be returned to the land, and everything would be fine once again; however, God says, "Hold on Daniel, I have a few things against your people before all will be made right." God told Daniel seventy weeks were determined against his people to accomplish this. To understand what is being said, we need to know what is meant by weeks. Israel observed two types of Sabbaths: every seventh day and every seventh year. If day was meant, the time period involved would be approximately one and a half years. Since nothing of scriptural significance was accomplished in that short period, the meaning could not be that this is weeks of days. The meaning is for that reason taken to be that weeks mean years, and seventy weeks of years would be 490 years. This also follows the following context, which will be explained.

God goes on to tell Daniel that when this period of time is complete, six things will have happened:

> Transgression will be finished.
> Sin will have ended.
> Atonement will have been made for iniquity.
> Everlasting righteousness will have been brought in.
> Vision and prophecy will be sealed.
> The most holy will be anointed.

When these things have happened, the completion of God's purposes for Daniel's people will have been accomplished; and Daniel's hopes for Israel will be complete.

> Seventy weeks have been decreed for your people
> and your holy city, to finish the transgression, to

make an end of sin, to make atonement for iniquity, to bring in everlasting righteousness, to seal up vision and prophecy and to anoint the most holy place. (Dan. 9:24)

This time period will begin, we are told, with a command/decree to restore and build Jerusalem. There are four decrees in scripture that have to do with the rebuilding of Jerusalem. Three of these have to do with the reconstruction of the temple. Only one decree has to do with the rebuilding of the city. This is the decree made in Nehemiah's days, made by King Artaxerxes of Persia, in his twentieth year.

Secular records state that Artaxerxes begin his reign n 465 BC, which would date the decree in Nehemiah 2 as 445 BC.

I (Nehemiah) said to the king, "Let the king live forever. Why should my face not be sad when the city, the place of my fathers' tombs, lies desolate and its gates have been consumed by fire?" Then the king said to me, "What would you request?" So I prayed to the God of heaven. I said to the king, "If it please the king, and if your servant has found favor before you, send me to Judah, to the city of my fathers' tombs, that I may rebuild it." Then the king said to me, the queen sitting beside him, "How long will your journey be, and when will you return?" So it pleased the king to send me, and I gave him a definite time. And I said to the king, "If it please the king, let letters be given me for the governors of the provinces beyond the River, that they may allow me to pass through until I come to Judah, and a letter to Asaph the keeper of the king's forest, that he may give me timber to make beams for the gates of the fortress which is by the temple, for the wall of the city and for the house to which I will go." And the king granted them to me because the good hand of my God was on me. (Neh. 2:3–8)

The period of seventy weeks (490 years) when God will be dealing with Daniel's people/Israel is divided into three sections. These divisions are made up of seven years (49 years), sixty-two weeks (434 years), and one remaining week, (7 years). We are told it/Jerusalem will be built again, with plaza and moat, even in times of distress (Daniel 9:25b). It took 49 years for Jerusalem to be rebuilt to the point of being again considered an established city. Those opposed to the rebuilding made the work difficult and caused much distress to the workers.

> Now when Sanballat, Tobiah, the Arabs, the Ammonites and the Ashdodites heard that the repair of the walls of Jerusalem went on, and that the breaches began to be closed, they were very angry. All of them conspired together to come and fight against Jerusalem and to cause a disturbance in it.
>
> Our enemies said, "They will not know or see until we come among them, kill them and put a stop to the work."
>
> From that day on, half of my (Nehemiah's) servants carried on the work while half of them held the spears, the shields, the bows and the breastplates; and the captains were behind the whole house of Judah. Those who were rebuilding the wall and those who carried burdens took their load with one hand doing the work and the other holding a weapon. As for the builders, each wore his sword girded at his side as he built, while the trumpeter stood near me. I said to the nobles, the officials and the rest of the people, "The work is great and extensive, and we are separated on the wall far from one another. At whatever place you hear the sound of the trumpet, rally to us there. Our God will fight for us." So we carried on the work with half of them holding spears from dawn until the stars appeared.

> At that time I also said to the people, "Let each man with his servant spend the night within Jerusalem so that they may be a guard for us by night and a laborer by day." So neither I, my brothers, my servants, nor the men of the guard who followed me, none of us removed our clothes, each took his weapon even to the water. (Neh. 4:7–8, 11, 16–23)

After the second period of sixty-two weeks (434 years), or a total of 483 years, we are told we come to Messiah the Prince. Here we must determine what is meant by the term "Messiah the Prince." Jesus lived approximately thirty-three years, and had an active ministry of three and a half years. During the years of His active ministry there were many efforts to make Him ruler of Israel, Messiah, and the king of the people. However, only once did Jesus offer Himself as Messiah. That is what is spoken of here by the phrase "Messiah the Prince." On that day the crowds met Him as He entered the city. They spread their cloaks and palm branches in the road before him. They shouted, "Hosanna to the Son of David; Blessed is He Who comes in the Name of the Lord, Hosanna in the highest!"

> When they had approached Jerusalem and had come to Bethphage, at the Mount of Olives, then Jesus sent two disciples, saying to them, "Go into the village opposite you, and immediately you will find a donkey tied there and a colt with her; untie them and bring them to Me. If anyone says anything to you, you shall say, 'The Lord has need of them,' and immediately he will send them." This took place to fulfill what was spoken through the prophet: "Say to the Daughter of Zion, 'Behold your King is coming to you, Gentle and mounted on a donkey, even on a colt, the foal of a beast of burden.'" The disciples went and did just as Jesus had instructed them, and brought the donkey and the colt, and laid their coats on them; and He sat on the coats. Most of the crowd spread their coats in

the road, and others were cutting branches from the trees and spreading them in the road. The crowds going ahead of Him, and those who followed, were shouting, "Hosanna to the Son of David; Blessed is He who comes in the Name of the Lord; Hosanna in the highest!" When He had entered Jerusalem, all the city was stirred, saying, "Who is this?" And the crowds were saying, "This is the prophet Jesus, from Nazareth in Galilee." (Matt. 21:1–11)

Because of this passage in Daniel, the religious leaders should have known the exact day their Messiah would be presented to them. Today we have some difficulty in determining that day for two reasons. We operate on the Roman calendar with 365 ¼ days in a year, rather than 360 days for the Jewish calendar. Secondly, our time changes from BC to AD; and the number of years that are involved in that turnover is uncertain. These two issues were not an issue with the Jewish leaders who should have been able to determine the exact date involved. We also know that they should have known the date by the fact that Jesus wept because they did not receive Him.

When He (Jesus) approached Jerusalem, He saw the city and wept over it, saying, "If you had known in this day, even you, the things which make for peace! But now they have been hidden from your eyes. For the days will come upon you when your enemies will throw up a barricade against you, and surround you and hem you in on every side, and they will level you to the ground and your children within you, and they will not leave in you one stone upon another, because you did not recognize the time of your visitation." (Luke 19:41–44)

At the end of the second period of 62 weeks and 483 years after the original decree and Messiah the Prince had been presented, we are told two things will happen. Messiah will be cut off and have nothing, and secondly the city of Jerusalem and the sanctuary (temple) would be destroyed. The cutting off of Messiah refers to the crucifixion of Jesus, which happened within a week of Jesus presenting Himself as Messiah. The excitement of His entry quickly passed and the shouting was replaced with cries, "Crucify Him!"

> But the chief priests and the elders persuaded the crowds to ask for Barabbas and to put Jesus to death. But the governor said to them, "Which of the two do you want me to release for you?" And they said, "Barabbas." Pilate said to them, "Then what shall I do with Jesus who is called Christ?" They all said, "Crucify Him!" And he said, "Why, what evil has He done?" But they kept shouting all the more, saying, "Crucify Him!" When Pilate saw that he was accomplishing nothing, but rather that a riot was starting, he took water and washed his hands in front of the crowd, saying, "I am innocent of this Man's blood; see to that yourselves." And all the people said, "His blood shall be on us and on our children!" (Matt. 27:20–25)

> Pilate then took Jesus and scourged Him. And the soldiers twisted together a crown of thorns and put it on His head, and put a purple robe on Him; and they began to come up to Him and say, "Hail, King of the Jews!" and to give Him slaps in the face. Pilate came out again and said to them, "Behold, I am bringing Him out to you so that you may know that I find no guilt in Him." Jesus then came out, wearing the crown of thorns and the purple robe. Pilate said to them, "Behold, the Man!" So when the chief priests and the officers saw Him, they cried out saying, "Crucify, crucify!" Pilate said to them, "Take Him yourselves and crucify Him, for I find no guilt in Him." The Jews answered him, "We have a law, and by that law He ought to die because He made Himself out to be the Son of

God." Therefore when Pilate heard this statement, he was even more afraid; and he entered into the Praetorium again and said to Jesus, "Where are You from?" But Jesus gave him no answer. So Pilate said to Him, "You do not speak to me? Do You not know that I have authority to release You, and I have authority to crucify You?" Jesus answered, "You would have no authority over Me, unless it had been given you from above; for this reason he who delivered Me to you has the greater sin." As a result of this Pilate made efforts to release Him, but the Jews cried out saying, "If you release this Man, you are no friend of Caesar; everyone who makes himself out to be a king opposes Caesar." Therefore when Pilate heard these words, he brought Jesus out, and sat down on the judgment seat at a place called The Pavement, but in Hebrew, Gabbatha. Now it was the day of preparation for the Passover; it was about the sixth hour. And he said to the Jews, "Behold, your King!" So they cried out, "Away with Him, away with Him, crucify Him!" Pilate said to them, "Shall I crucify your King?" The chief priests answered, "We have no king but Caesar." So he then handed Him over to him to be crucified. (John 19:1–16)

Daniel's Prophecy states that Messiah would be cut off, but in addition it says He will have nothing. Our Lord was promised much by the Father, if He would come into the world to be our Savior. At the cross He suffered the death we all deserve, but died with nothing, not having received anything that had been promised. He received no glory only humiliation, Oh but wait there will be a second advent of our Savior.

The second thing predicted in Daniel prophecy to happen after the end of the sixty-ninth week, was the destruction of Jerusalem and the temple. This occurred about 38 years after Jesus presented Himself and after the sixty-ninth week, when the Roman General Titus besieged and destroyed Jerusalem in 70 AD. This was much longer the seven years of the prophesied seventieth week. This causes some problems of interpretation that will be explained in a coming chapter.

The remainder of this section of Daniel chapter 9 speak of *the end*, which refers to the end times, which are yet to occur and will also be explained in a later chapter.

God always has His man, and at the time of Judah's captivity, Daniel was that man. Being a person serving in Nebuchadnezzar's court, he certainly did much to safeguard his people during the captivity. When Babylon fell to Medo-Persia, Daniel again rose to a high position in the court Of Darius, and must have had connections with Cyrus. Undoubtedly he was instrumental is the return of the captives to their land. Daniel's readings foretold what would happen to the nations that the Israelites were subject to during the Persian and Greek Empires. Knowing what would happen had to be an encouragement to Daniel's people, for in spite of suffering, they knew God was in control. Beyond past history, Daniel's prophecies stretch into the future for us. We to can know God is still in control. Daniel stood for God in difficult times. His stand has impacted people for God throughout the ages. God is still looking for men and women who will stand for Him. Will you be a Daniel in our days?

MESSIAH THE PRINCE CHAP. 12

Through human history, mankind has been locked in a spiritual war. This war began in the distant past when Lucifer became dissatisfied with his position before God. Thinking God was not fair, he set out to take over for God, saying, "I will ascend above the heights of the clouds; I will make myself like the Most High" (Isa. 14:14). As we have seen in chapter 3, God countered Lucifer's (now the Devil and Satan) attack with a new order of personal beings. Satan was quick to realize that this man and woman placed into his world were not friends, and set out to win them over. He used the same attack that caused his own downfall. He caused them to question God, and to believe there was more to be had then what God was allowing them to have. Deception works best with a weaker vessel, so he approached Eve, who listened to him rather than heeding God's earlier commands. It seems at that point Adam chose to follow Eve rather than God, the fall was complete and Satan had accomplished a major victory. Fortunately God's plan for the Human race included a plan of redemption, not included in the creation of Spiritual beings/angels. The first mention of this plan is that it would be accomplished though "the seed of the woman" (Gen. 3:15).

God's plan of redemption was not an afterthought, but it was in the mind and workings of God from the very beginning. It seems that

God the Father and God the Son agreed in working out this plan of redemption—that if the Son would enter the human race and become the redeemer, the Father would give "Him (Jesus)" all those who believed the Son and accepted the salvation provided.

> Father, I desire that they also, whom You have given Me, be with Me where I am, so that they may see My glory which You have given Me, for You loved Me before the foundation of the world. (John 17:24)

> He chose us in Him/Christ before the foundation of the world, that we would be holy and blameless before Him. In love. (Eph. 1:4)

> For we who have believed enter that rest, just as He has said, "As I swore in My wrath, They shall not enter My rest," although His works were finished from the foundation of the world. (Heb. 4:3)

> Otherwise, He would have needed to suffer often since the foundation of the world; but now once at the consummation of the ages He has been manifested to put away sin by the sacrifice of Himself. (Heb. 9:26)

> For He was foreknown before the foundation of the world, but has appeared in these last times for the sake of you. (1 Pet. 1:20)

All those who believed would be given to the Son, and He would be made the ruler of the nations from which they came. The Son would not only be a king, but "The King of Kings." God, the Father, scoffs at all those who try to take the rule of the nations of the world into their own hand with disregard for Him.

> Why are the nations in an uproar and the peoples devising a vain thing? The kings of the earth take their stand and the rulers take counsel together

against the Lord and against His Anointed, saying, "Let us tear their fetters apart and cast away their cords from us!" He who sits in the heavens laughs, The Lord scoffs at them. Then He will speak to them in His anger and terrify them in His fury, saying, "But as for Me, I have installed My King upon Zion, My holy mountain." "I will surely tell of the decree of the Lord: He said to Me, 'You are My Son, today I have begotten You. 'Ask of Me, and I will surely give the nations as Your inheritance, and the very ends of the earth as Your possession. (Ps. 2:1–8)

To Accomplish His plan, God chose to use two men, Abraham and David. From the descendants of Abraham He built a nation to work through. From David, God chose a family and line through which He would bring forth the one, who was to be king. A person does not have to look very far to see where Satan will concentrate his attacks. First of all he is seeking to wipe out the human race. It was man, who God put in the Garden of Eden to gain dominion with the purpose of restoring the creation affects by Satan fall and disobedience. Secondly Satan especially hates the Nation of Israel and the Jewish people, because it is through them that God has purposed to carry out a majority of His plans. Thirdly Satan is out to make shipwreck of the line of David, which is the kingly/Messianic line, for it is though David's line that the king/ redeemer was promised. This person will be given final rule, the rule that Satan desires for himself.

As we left the last chapter, Satan must have felt pretty smug. Human death was rampant, the nation Israel was in captivity, banished from the Promised Land, and the kingly line appeared to have been brought to an end. It would have appeared Satan was gaining an upper hand, but our God always has control in governing the courses of His creation. It is now time to see how He will correct the affairs of world happenings to overcome Satan's onslaughts.

In God's plan to correct the sin problem, He had created a new order of personal life, but the first humans succumbed to Satan's tempting, and became part of the sin problem. Sin has engulfed the entire human race. Sin is hereditary passed on from the first human parents as a result of their disobedience and having been placed under a curse. Today people sin because they are sinners with a sin nature. God told the first couple, that if they ate from the tree of the knowledge of good and evil they would die. He has also said "the wages of sin is death" (Rom. 3:20). The problem for humanity was that every individual had the price of sin, death, hanging over their heads. If another paid the price for himself he was dead, and forever separated from God. Not only could he/she not help himself or herself, they also could not help anyone else. A redeemer was needed who was not part of the sin problem.

We have seen that God had the problem worked out from the foundations of the world, in that God, the Son, agreed to enter the human race in order to become the redeemer of the world. Still there was one problem, how could this happen without the redeemer becoming part of the sin problem.

Fortunately God had control of this difficulty, and has already given us the answer, "the seed of the woman" (Gen. 3:15). We, however, need to understand what this means. It is normal to speak of the continuance of the human race by "the seed of the man," but in Genesis 3:15, it speaks of the seed as "the seed of the woman." It seems that because Eve was deceived, and Adam sinned willfully in following Eve, that the sin nature has been passed on through the male; therefore, just as through one man sin entered into the world, and death through sin, and so death spread to all men, because all sinned (Rom. 5:12). Everyone that has been born after Adam and Eve's sin has received a sin nature passed off from father to child. For Jesus to come into the world and take upon himself, humanity, if He was to be the redeemer, He could not be a part of the sin problem, and therefore He could not get his humanity from a human father. When we understand the term, "the seed of the woman" we also understand that God always understood how He would provide a sinless Savior. Jesus got His humanity from His mother, and being conceived by the Holy Spirit, He had no human father.

> Now in the sixth month the angel Gabriel was sent by God to a city of Galilee named Nazareth,

to a virgin betrothed to a man whose name was Joseph, of the house of David. The virgin's name was Mary. And having come in, the angel said to her, "Rejoice, highly favored one, the Lord is with you; blessed are you among women!" But when she saw him, she was troubled at his saying, and considered what manner of greeting this was. Then the angel said to her, "Do not be afraid, Mary, for you have found favor with God. And behold, you will conceive in your womb and bring forth a Son, and shall call His name Jesus. He will be great, and will be called the Son of the Highest, and the Lord God will give Him the throne of His father David. And He will reign over the house of Jacob forever, and of His kingdom there will be no end." Then Mary said to the angel, "How can this be, since I do not know a man?" And the angel answered and said to her, "The Holy Spirit will come upon you, and the power of the Highest will overshadow you; therefore, also, that Holy One who is to be born will be called the Son of God. (Luke 1:26–35)

Today the thought of a virgin birth is scoffed at as being physically impossible; however, all things are possible with God as Jesus said, "With people this is impossible, but with God all things are possible" (Matt. 19:26). Not only is a virgin birth possible with God, it is essential for a sinless Savior and the redemption of men and women. In Jesus, God Himself (God the Son) became a perfect human being. Being sinless and not part of the sin problem, He did not need to die for Himself, but could die for us. Being the God-Man His death was of infinite value, and covered the sins of the entire world. We were the sinners, we should have been on the cross, but he was there for each one of us. When we accept His death for us, God sees us as being "In Christ" and counts us as righteous as the Lord Jesus Himself. He (God) made Him (Christ) who knew no sin to be sin on our behalf, so that we might become the righteousness of God in Him (2 Cor. 5:21).

We have been left with a second problem—that we now need to see how God has worked it out. King David was promised that one of his descendants would sit on his throne forever. At the time of the captivity in chapter 11, when Jehoiachin, the grandson of Josiah the last recognized King of Judah, was carried into captivity; it was pronounced by Jeremiah that he would be childless as having one of his descendants sit on the throne of David.

> "As I live," declares the Lord, "even though Coniah [Jehoichin] the son of Jehoiakim king of Judah were a signet ring on My right hand, yet I would pull you off; and I will give you over into the hand of those who are seeking your life, yes, into the hand of those whom you dread, even into the hand of Nebuchadnezzar king of Babylon and into the hand of the Chaldeans. I will hurl you and your mother who bore you into another country where you were not born, and there you will die. But as for the land to which they desire to return, they will not return to it. "Is this man Coniah [Jehoiachin] a despised, shattered jar? Or is he an undesirable vessel? Why have he and his descendants been hurled out and cast into a land that they had not known? O land, land, land. Hear the word of the Lord! "Thus says the Lord, 'Write this man down childless, a man who will not prosper in his days; for no man of his descendants will prosper sitting on the throne of David or ruling again in Judah.'"
> (Jer. 22:24–30)

Certainly Satan must have thought he had won a great victory. In desiring to be like God, he surely wanted his man to be king, and now from all appearances he had been able to bring an end to the line of David, the kingly line. Only thing again in chapter 11, at the end of the 69th week of Daniel, we saw that Messiah the Prince would be presented. Let us now see how this was to be made possible, and how God was still going to keep His promise to David, that one of his descendants would sit on his throne forever.

Although Jehoiachin was pronounced as being childless concerning having a child who would sit on the throne of David, he was not childless, and seems to have had a son in captivity. We see this in the genealogy of Matthew's gospel.

> The record of the genealogy of Jesus the Messiah, the son of David, the son of Abraham: Abraham was the father of Isaac, Isaac the father of Jacob, and Jacob the father of Judah and his brothers. Judah was the father of Perez and Zerah by Tamar, Perez was the father of Hezron, and Hezron the father of Ram. Ram was the father of Amminadab, Amminadab the father of Nahshon, and Nahshon the father of Salmon. Salmon was the father of Boaz by Rahab, Boaz was the father of Obed by Ruth, and Obed the father of Jesse. Jesse was the father of David the king. David was the father of Solomon by Bathsheba who had been the wife of Uriah. Solomon was the father of Rehoboam, Rehoboam the father of Abijah, and Abijah the father of Asa. Asa was the father of Jehoshaphat, Jehoshaphat the father of Joram, and Joram the father of Uzziah. Uzziah was the father of Jotham, Jotham the father of Ahaz, and Ahaz the father of Hezekiah. Hezekiah was the father of Manasseh, Manasseh the father of Amon, and Amon the father of Josiah. Josiah became the father of Jeconiah/Coniah/Jehoiachin (three names of the same person) and his brothers, at the time of the deportation to Babylon. After the deportation to Babylon: Jeconiah became the father of Shealtiel, and Shealtiel the father of Zerubbabel. Zerubbabel was the father of Abihud, Abihud the father of Eliakim, and Eliakim the father of Azor. Azor was the father of Zadok, Zadok the father of Achim, and Achim the father of Eliud. Eliud was

the father of Eleazar, Eleazar the father of Matthan, and Matthan the father of Jacob. Jacob was the father of Joseph the husband of Mary, by whom Jesus was born, who is called the Messiah. (Matt. 1:1–16)

In writing his gospel, Matthew is writing to Jews. One of the main purposes in writing is to show that Jesus is their promised Messiah. In Matthew Gospel we have the genealogy of the kings of Israel, beginning with Abraham, the patriarch of the nation Israel, through King David. This genealogy ends with Joseph, the Virgin Mary's husband. Now let's look at the genealogy in Luke's gospel. Luke was a Doctor, and in his gospel he stresses the physical nature of Jesus, showing Jesus as the Son of Man. For this reason Luke carries his genealogy back to Adam, to show the manhood of Jesus.

When He began His ministry, Jesus Himself was about thirty years of age, being, as was supposed, the son of Joseph, the son of Eli, the son of Matthat, the son of Levi, the son of Melchi, the son of Jannai, the son of Joseph, the son of Mattathias, the son of Amos, the son of Nahum, the son of Hesli, the son of Naggai, the son of Maath, the son of Mattathias, the son of Semein, the son of Josech, the son of Joda, the son of Joanan, the son of Rhesa, the son of Zerubbabel, the son of Shealtiel, the son of Neri, the son of Melchi, the son of Addi, the son of Cosam, the son of Elmadam, the son of Er, the son of Joshua, the son of Eliezer, the son of Jorim, the son of Matthat, the son of Levi, the son of Simeon, the son of Judah, the son of Joseph, the son of Jonam, the son of Eliakim, the son of Melea, the son of Menna, the son of Mattatha, the son of Nathan, the son of David, the son of Jesse, the son of Obed, the son of Boaz, the son of Salmon, the son of Nahshon, the son of Amminadab, the son of Ram, the son of Hezron, the son of Perez, the son of Judah, the son of Jacob, the son of Isaac, the son of Abraham, the son of Terah, the son of Nahor, the son of Serug, the son of Reu, the son of Peleg, the son of Heber, the son of Shelah, the son of Cainan, the son of Arphaxad, the son of Shem, the son of Noah, the son of Lamech, the son of Methuselah, the son of Enoch, the son of Jared, the son of Mahalaleel, the son of Cainan, the son of Enosh, the son of Seth, the son of Adam, the son of God. (Luke 3:23–38)

Three things that are highlighted in the genealogies need to be considered. First, Matthew's genealogy ends with Joseph, the husband of Mary. Joseph was a descendant of David through the kingly line, but Mary was not; however, as the adapted son of Joseph, Jesus had all the rights of a natural born son, which in this case included a right to the throne of David. Looking at Luke's genealogy, we are told that Jesus was supposed to be the son of Joseph. He was not the physical son of Joseph, but the adopted son, as we have seen. Going on in Luke's genealogy we see that Mary's lineage does go back to David, but through Nathan rather than Solomon. In conclusion, we see that in Jesus, His physical being goes back to David through His mother Mary, but His legal right to the throne of David through Joseph his adopted father. Satan may have though he had ended the Messianic line, but we see that our God is way ahead of him. Our God is a God of the impossible, He not only keeps his promises, but He is able to work His final end in spite of all types of opposition.

The Messiah Prince presented Himself at the exact time in accordance with Daniel's prophecy. However, His people Israel did not receive Him, and rather had him crucified. After Jesus was crucified Joseph of Arimathea having asked for the Lord's body, along with Nicodemus, prepared the Lord's body for burial.

Then the Jews, because it was the day of preparation, so that the bodies would not remain on the cross on the Sabbath (for that Sabbath was a high day), asked Pilate that their legs might be broken, and that they might be taken away. So the soldiers came, and broke the legs of the first man and of the other who was crucified with Him; but coming to Jesus, when they saw that He was already dead, they did not break His legs. But one of the soldiers pierced His side with a spear, and immediately blood and water came out. And he who has seen has testified, and his testimony is true; and he knows that he is telling the truth, so that you also may believe. For these things came to pass to fulfill the Scripture, "Not a bone of Him shall be broken." And again another Scripture says, "They shall look on Him whom they pierced." After these things Joseph of Arimathea, being a disciple of Jesus, but a secret one for fear of the Jews, asked Pilate that he might take away the body of Jesus; and Pilate granted permission. So he came and took away His body. Nicodemus, who had first come to Him by night, also came, bringing a mixture of myrrh and aloes, about a hundred pounds weight. So they took the body of Jesus and bound it in linen wrappings with the spices, as is the burial custom of the Jews. Now in the place where He was crucified there was a garden, and in the garden a new tomb in which no one had yet been laid. Therefore because of the Jewish day of preparation, since the tomb was nearby, they laid Jesus there. (John 19:31–42)

With Jesus dead and buried, Satan must have thought he had won a great victory, stumping out the supposed savior of the world. Three days later we see the real truth. The tomb was empty and Jesus was said to be alive. God had won again, and in addition to a victory over Satan the defeat of Death.

Now after the Sabbath, as it began to dawn toward the first day of the week, Mary Magdalene and the other Mary came to look at the grave. And behold, a severe earthquake had occurred, for an angel of the Lord descended from heaven and came and rolled away the stone and sat upon it. And his appearance was like lightning, and his clothing as white as snow. The guards shook for fear of him and became like dead men. The angel said to the women, "Do not be afraid; for I know that you are looking for Jesus who has been crucified. He is not here, for He has risen, just as He said. Come; see the place where He was lying. Go quickly and tell His disciples that He has risen from the dead. (Matt. 28:1–7)

Mary Magdalene was quick to obey the angel, and went and told the disciples.

Now on the first day of the week Mary Magdalene came early to the tomb, while it was still dark, and saw the stone already taken away from the tomb. So she ran and came to Simon Peter and to the other disciple whom Jesus loved, and said to them, "They have taken away the Lord out of the tomb, and we do not know where they have laid Him." So Peter and the other disciple went forth, and they were going to the tomb. The two were running together; and the other disciple ran ahead faster than Peter and came to the tomb first; and stooping and looking in, he saw the linen wrappings lying there; but he did not go in. And so Simon Peter also came, following him, and entered the tomb; and he saw the linen wrappings lying there, and the face-cloth which had been on His head, not lying with the linen wrappings, but rolled up in a place by itself. So the other disciple who had first come to the tomb then also entered, and he saw and believed. For as yet they did not understand the Scripture, that He must rise again from the dead. (John 20:1–9)

It is amazing that after three and a half years with the Lord, and the many times that He told the disciples that He must die, be crucified, and rise from the dead, that they still did not understand. Coming to the tomb, Peter and John were caused to believe. Let's discuss what they saw. They saw the grave clothes and the linen cloth placed over the Lord's face rolled up, but what they saw was unusual. The grave clothes had been wrapped around the Lord's body with intermingled layers of myrrh and aloes. This had glued the linen cloth together to form sort of a cocoon around the Lord's body. What Peter and John saw was the cocoon still in tack, but the Lord's body gone. It was said the body was stolen, but this could never have happened with the grave clothes left in tack and empty of the body. The only answer was resurrection. The face cloth was rolled up. The one who did this had to be alive. YES, the Lord was alive, and what Peter and John saw caused them to believe. We have no other answer to the empty tomb, but to also believe.

Jesus presented Himself as Messiah, but He was rejected. Now we must wait until He comes again, when He will again present Himself as King.

WHAT HAPPENED TO DANIEL'S SEVENTIETH WEEK

CHAP. 13

We left chapter 11 at the end of Daniel's 69th week, when Messiah the Prince was presented to the nation of Israel and rejected. Now we need to consider the 70th week of Daniel's prophecy. As we have seen, this is a week of years or seven years. There are two views concerning this 70th week: The first is that all the seventy weeks follow each other in continuous sequence. The second is that there is a time gap between the 69th and 70th week.

Let's first consider the first view. Two things are said to happen after the 69th week. Messiah will be cut off and Jerusalem will be destroyed. Messiah/Christ was cut off/crucified the same week He offered himself as Messiah. Jerusalem was destroyed by the Roman army led by General Titus in 70 AD, which was 37 or 38 years after the crucifixion, and much longer than seven years. Looking at history at that time nothing of prophetic significance happened within the next seven years. God also told Daniel at the end of the 70 weeks (490 years) six things would happen. These six things were already noted in chapter 11, but we will repeat them again.

Transgression will be finished.

Sin will have ended.

Atonement will have been made for iniquity.

Everlasting righteousness will have been brought in.

Vision and prophecy will be sealed.

The most holy will be anointed.

At the present time none of these six things have happened. We must then assume we have not come to the end of the 70th week of Daniel's prophecy. This being the case we need to look into the possibility of a time gap between the 69th and 70th week of Daniel's prophecy.

Many people would not accept a time gap here, but time gaps in the Bible are common. Events about Christ in the Old Testament are often seen as happening together, but some happened at His first advent and others will happen at His second advent. This is a time gap already of nearly 2000 years. Another good example of a gap in scripture is seen on the occasion when Jesus read scripture at the synagogue in Nazareth.

> And He came to Nazareth, where He had been brought up; and as was His custom, He entered the synagogue on the Sabbath, and stood up to read. And the book of the prophet Isaiah was handed to Him. And He opened the book and found the place where it was written, The Spirit of the Lord is upon Me, because He anointed Me to preach the Gospel to the poor. He has sent Me to proclaim release to the captives, and recovery of sight to the blind. To set free those who are oppressed, to proclaim the favorable year of the Lord." And He closed the book, gave it back to the attendant and sat down; and the eyes of all in the synagogue were fixed on Him. And He began to say to them, "Today this Scripture has been fulfilled in your hearing." (Luke 4:16–21)

After reading Jesus told those listening, that the things prophesied by Isaiah were being fulfilled in their hearing. The very things Jesus was doing were fulfilling what was spoken by Isaiah.

> The Spirit of the Lord God is upon me, Because the Lord has anointed me To bring good news to the afflicted; He has sent me to bind up the broken-hearted, To proclaim liberty to captives and freedom to prisoners; To proclaim the favorable year of the Lord and the day of vengeance of our God. (Isa. 61:1–2)

Here we must note that Jesus did not quote the end of the Isaiah passage He read from. He left out "the day of vengeance of our God." Why did He do this? The reason was that He only read what was happening in that day. The vengeance of God will occur at His second advent, and did not occur at His first coming. Here in one verse we have a time gap of already nearly 2000 years. Time gaps are not unreasonable in scripture, and it seems that this is what we have between the 69th and 70th week of Daniel's prophecy.

> Now we need to explain why God would allow such a time gap. God chose the descendants of Abraham, Isaac, and Jacob to be His people. For you are a holy people to the Lord your God; the Lord your God has chosen you to be a people for His own possession out of all the peoples who are on the face of the earth (Deut. 7:6).

Often the Israelites have mistaken being called God's chosen people to be a free ticket to heaven. This, however, was not why God chose them. God chose them to be a people through whom He would accomplish His purposes. A people through whom: (1) He would bring forth His revelation to the world, (2) He would bring forth a Savior through the nation Israel, and (3) a nation to take the message of salvation to the world. The first purpose was accomplished in that the scriptures with the possible exceptions of Job and Luke were written by Jews. Secondly Jesus our Savior was a Jew. This purpose of God was easily accomplished by Israel being fruitful and multiplying. A few Jews have carried God's message to others, but this has not been largely the case; in fact, Jews have looked down on Gentiles, even calling them dogs. When the Jews were disobedient to the calling to take the gospel to the nations—even to the degree of having their own Messiah crucified— God set them aside. In setting Israel aside, God has chosen anyone who will accept Jesus as His gospel messengers.

After Christ's ascension, God send His Holy Spirit on all believers. On the day of Pentecost (Acts 2:1–4), He began building His Church, the Body of Christ. Jesus was no longer on earth carrying God's message, and the Church, empowered by the Holy Spirit, became Christ's arms, legs, and mouthpieces to carry the gospel to others.

Today there are many who say God is through with Israel and who will finish His work through the Church. The Apostle Paul would disagree with this thought.

> I say then, God has not rejected His people, has He? May it never be! For I too am an Israelite, a descendant of Abraham, of the tribe of Benjamin. God has not rejected His people whom He foreknew....
> I say then, they did not stumble so as to fall, did they? May it never be! But by their transgression salvation has come to the Gentiles, to make them jealous. Now if their transgression is riches for the world and their failure is riches for the Gentiles, how much more will their fulfillment be! (Rom. 11:1–2b, 11–12)

What God plans and begins, He always finishes. This is also true of Israel, what He begin with Israel He will finish with Israel. This is also true of all believers. What He started with you and me He will also finish. "For I am confident of this very thing, that He who began a good work in you will perfect it until the day of Christ Jesus (Philippians 1:6). Yes, there is a day coming when God will have completed His work for the church. At that time He will call the church home to be with Him.

But we do not want you to be uninformed, brethren, about those who are asleep, so that you will not grieve as do the rest who have no hope. For if we believe that Jesus died and rose again, even so God will bring with Him those who have fallen asleep in Jesus. For this we say to you by the word of the Lord, that we, who are alive and remain until the coming of the Lord, will not precede those who have fallen asleep. For the Lord Himself will descend from heaven with a shout, with the voice of the archangel and with the trumpet of God, and the dead in Christ will rise first. Then we who are alive and remain will be caught up together with them in the clouds to meet the Lord in the air, and so we shall always be with the Lord. Therefore comfort one another with these words. (1 Thess. 4:13–18)

After God has completed His work through the Church, He will then finish His work with Israel. Looking back at Daniel's seventy weeks, God said this period of time had to do with Daniel's people/Israel. We have seen that that week has never occurred. Now it is time to look at that seventieth week, and see how God deals with Israel, to complete the work He has called them to do.

DANIEL'S SEVENTIETH WEEK   CHAP. 14

We have seen that in God's dealing with Daniel's people over the prophesied seventy week period, that the period of sixty-nine weeks took us to Messiah the Prince presenting Himself. After this event we saw there was a time gap, when God worked through the church. During this time gap and after the 69th week, we are told that two things happened; then after seven weeks and the sixty-two weeks (69 weeks total), the Messiah will be cut off and have nothing; and the people of the prince who is to come will destroy the city and the sanctuary (Dan. 9:26a). The remaining events of Daniel's prophecy involve great destruction; it says, "Desolations are determined." We have already seen in earlier chapters that with the completion of the seventy weeks all things will be set right, which is not the picture we see here. These events of destruction must thus happen before the seventy weeks are complete, and the only time this is possible is during the 70th week.

To understand what is happening here at the end of Daniel's prophecy, we must identify the prince of the people, "the people of the prince who is to come will destroy the city and the sanctuary" (Dan. 9:26a). There are those that say we have only one prince here and the prince in verse 26 refers back to Messiah the Prince in verse 25. From History we know Jerusalem and the temple were destroyed by the Romans in 70 AD, thus the prince of the people would have to be Roman. Messiah the Prince was Jesus who was a Jew. The coming of this prince of the people is said to be at the end. This would make his coming during the 70th week of Daniel, and after the time of the Church and the removal of the Church to heaven. Making this time still future.

We have continually spoken of spiritual warfare, and here we seem to have this warfare intensified, as Satan makes a supreme effort to eliminate God's people, Israel. It does not take much imagination to see that this prince is Satan's number one man who is spoken of throughout scripture.

> While I was contemplating the horns, behold, another horn, a little one, came up among them, and three of the first horns were pulled out by the roots before it; and behold, this horn possessed eyes like the eyes of a man and a mouth uttering great boasts. (Dan. 7:8)

> Let no one in any way deceive you, for it/our gathering together to Christ will not come unless the apostasy comes first, and the man of lawlessness is revealed, the son of destruction, who opposes and exalts himself above every so-called god or object of worship, so that he takes his seat in the temple of God, displaying himself as being god. (2 Thess. 2:3–4)

> Who is the liar but the one who denies that Jesus is the Christ? This is the antichrist, the one who denies the Father and the Son. (1 John 2:22)

> And the beast, which I saw, was like a leopard, and his feet were like those of a bear, and his mouth like the mouth of a lion. And the dragon gave him his power and his throne and great authority. (Rev. 13:2)

Above are only a few references to this one, who is often spoken of as "The Antichrist," who scripture says will appear in the last days. Satan is a master counterfeiter, and this individual is likely his best work, an effort to counterfeit God's son. Daniel's prophecy states that to the end there will be war; desolations are determined. Satan will use this individual in his attempt to wipe out God's people (Israel).

Many would ask how a loving God would allow this individual to come and bring such destruction. Let us list some possible reasons.

Satan has said God is not fair and is set out to be like the Most High (Isa. 14:14). It seems that God will allow Satan to prove how wrong he is by allowing him to bring destruction and destroying all that is good.

Often one has to be brought to an end of themselves and their pride before they will turn to God. The addict after ruining his life by trying everything for fulfillment will turn to God as a last resort. It seems this is the case with Israel. They have prided themselves in their own righteousness and turned from God. Throughout scripture God has called them a stiff-necked people. God has plans and purpose for Israel, and He is not going to give up on them. It will take some very hard times for Israel to turn to God, but this will happen in this seven-year period.

How can God allow such hurting to happen to people? God is a God of justice and must deal with sin; however even in judgment God is merciful. This time will be a time of great revival, when during these difficult times many will turn to Christ. Satan's Antichrist will demand worship, and many who refuse will be martyred, but God says though they died they have the victory. Why? They are in heaven! How many are there, let's look at scripture and see a vision the Apostle John had of heaven.

> After these things I looked, and behold, a great multitude which no one could count, from every nation and all tribes and peoples and tongues, standing before the throne and before the Lamb, clothed in white robes, and palm branches were in their hands; and they cry out with a loud voice, saying, "Salvation to our God who sits on the

throne, and to the Lamb." And all the angels were standing round the throne and around the elders and the four living creatures; and they fell on their faces before the throne and worshiped God saying, "Amen, blessing and glory and wisdom and thanksgiving and honor and power and might, be to our God forever and ever. Amen." Then one of the elders answered, saying to me, "These who are clothed in the white robes, who are they, and where have they come from?" I said to him, "My lord, you know." And he said to me, "These are the ones who come out the great tribulation, and they have washed their robes and made them white in the blood of the Lamb. For this reason, they are before the throne of God; and they serve Him day and night in His temple; and He who sits on the throne will spread His tabernacle over them. They will hunger no longer, nor thirst anymore; nor will the sun beat down on them, nor any heat; for the Lamb in the center of the throne will be their shepherd, and will guide them to springs of the water of life; and God will wipe every tear from their eyes." (Rev. 7:9–16)

How many are there? So many that they can't be counted—a great multitude. Where did they come from? They came out of the great tribulation. Yes, God is a loving God; He is about getting people to heaven, and sometimes He takes drastic steps to accomplish His purposes.

Back to Daniel's prophecy, we need do look at some of the things that will happen. In verse 27, we see this prince will make a covenant with many for one week or for seven years. We are dealing with Daniel's people, so this covenant is with the Jews. Since Israel was formed as a nation in 1948 there has been conflict over the possession of the land between Israel and the Palestinians, who have been joined with the Arab nations. This has resulted in continuous negotiations to find a settlement. No answers to the conflict have been found, and the Arabs believe the only answer is the eradication of Israel. This prince will have great oral ability, which he will use to deceive many.

> This horn possessed eyes like the eyes of a man and a mouth uttering great boasts. (Dan. 7:8)

> There was given to him a mouth speaking arrogant words and blasphemies, and authority to act for forty-two months was given to him. And he opened his mouth in blasphemies against God, to blaspheme His name and His tabernacle, that is, those who dwell in heaven. (Rev. 13:5–6)

Where many have failed this person given satanic ability will be able to negotiate a covenant of peace in the Middle East, which Israel will agree to. With the Church being caught up to be with the Lord, the restraint of the indwelling Holy Spirit in Christians will have been removed and this prince will gain a major place in world affairs.

> For the mystery of lawlessness is already at work; only he who now restrains will do so until he is taken out of the way. Then that lawless one will be revealed whom the Lord will slay with the breath of His mouth and bring to an end by the appearance of His coming; that is, the one whose coming is in accord with the activity of Satan, with all power and signs and false wonders, and with all the deception of wickedness for those who perish, because they did not receive the love of the truth so as to be saved. (2 Thess. 2:7–10)

This prince is a silver tongued, power gabbler, and like many political figures, he will tell the people what they want to hear until he is in power and control. He will come on the scene at the beginning of this seven-year period. He uses the first three and a half years to rise in power. We can see his power to influence people in that he is able to make a covenant with Israel, seemingly quieting the Middle East problem; where over the years many have failed. "And he will make a firm covenant with the many for one week" (Dan. 9:27a). Like many others in the political arena, once in power the prince fails to keep his commitments. Once in power in the middle of the week, after three and a half years the prince breaks his covenant and stops the Jewish sacrifice; "but in the middle of the week he will put a stop to sacrifice and grain offering" (Dan. 9:27b). Why? We have seen earlier that Satan wants to be "like the Most High." At this point it seems Satan's Antichrist says, "Stop all worship, I am God worship me." Although we are not told so, he most likely not only stops the Jewish sacrifice he also probably tries to stop all worship, but that of himself. The Lord Jesus foretold of this time. Antichrist demanding worship and setting himself up in God's temple as God is the abomination of desolation told of by Daniel.

> "Therefore when you see the abomination of desolation which was spoken of through Daniel the prophet, standing in the holy place (let the reader understand), then those who are in Judea must flee to the mountains. Whoever is on the housetop must not go down to get the things out that are in his house. Whoever is in the field must not turn back to get his cloak. But woe to those who are pregnant and to those who are nursing babies in those days! But pray that your flight will not be in the winter, or on a Sabbath. For then there will be a great tribulation, such as has not occurred since the beginning of the world until now, nor ever will. Unless those days had been cut short, no life would have been saved; but for the sake of the elect those days will be cut short. (Matt. 24:15–22)

When this time comes and Antichrist is in control; the Lord exhorts those in Judah to flee to the Mountains for their own safety. Most likely this refers to the mountainous area across the Jordan River.

Daniel goes on to say the end will come with a flood of desolation, and this prince will bring desolation resulting in complete destruction, until destruction is poured out on this desolator. What we see happening in Daniel's seventieth week correlates with the Book of Revelation. Let's turn to Revelation for a more complete picture of this period. The Apostle John is told what to write in this book, which gives us an outline of the book and helps us to understand what John has written. "Therefore, write the things which you have seen, and the things which are, and the things which will take place after these things (Rev. 1:19). This is a three-point outline of the entire book that John is told to write.

The things which you have seen. What John saw was a vision of Christ, which he records in chapter 1.

The things that are. John was living in the beginning of the Church Age; and in chapters 2 and 3, we see descriptions of the Church.

The things which will take place after these things. From chapter 4 to 22 of the Book of Revelation discusses things that will happen after the Church Age. Believers of the Church are still here, which tells us the remainder of the book is still to happen in the future.

We have seen earlier that the seventieth week of Daniel will begin after the Church is taken up to be with the Lord; therefore, much of the Book of Revelation discusses this seven-year period. In chapter 19 of Revelation, we see a vision of heaven followed by the second advent of Christ to earth. We must thus conclude that chapters 4 to 18 of Revelation occur during the seventieth week of Daniel, a period also called the Tribulation.

God has promised Christ that He will rule the nations (Psalm 2). Satan, the great counterfeiter wants this for his man, Antichrist. For a short time it seems Satan is able to pull this off. We have seen that a time is coming when Antichrist will demand to be worshipped, and will have worldwide influence. He seems to also control the world's economy at this time; allowing only certain individuals to buy and sell.

> And he causes all, the small and the great, and the rich and the poor, and the free men and the slaves, to be given a mark on their right hand or on their forehead, and he provides that no one will be able to buy or to sell, except the one who has the mark, either the name of the beast or the number of his name. (Rev. 13:16)

With Antichrist's control in world affairs, the destruction foretold by Daniel accelerates. Many deny that the Book of Revelation can be taken literally, saying a loving God would not allow such devastation, and hurt to people; however, John was instructed to write what he saw.

> I was in the Spirit on the Lord's day, and I heard behind me a loud voice like the sound of a trumpet saying, "Write in a book what you see, and send it to the seven churches. (Rev. 1:10–11a)

What John saw in a vision was the actual events that will occur on earth during this seven years period. What John saw might be compared to what we would see, if we were watching a war movie. He saw things that actually will happen. Yes, the descriptions John uses in Revelation are unusual, but we need to remember John was living in the first century AD. He used the terms of his day to describe what will still happen in our future. This spiritual warfare is terrible and it will get worse, in spite of many saying God would never allow this to happen.

We need to see another reason for this awful destruction. Satan has had access to heaven where he has accused us believers before God. There is a time coming when he will be cast out of heaven for the last time. Most likely this will happen at the middle of the seven-year period, when Antichrist calls to be worshipped. Satan too desires to be worshipped, and many think that at this time Satan will take possession of the Antichrist to the point that he becomes Satan incarnate, which would explain the great abilities of Antichrist.

> And there was war in heaven, Michael and his angels waging war with the dragon. The dragon and his angels waged war, and they were not strong enough, and there was no longer a place found for them in heaven. And the great dragon was thrown down, the serpent of old who is called the devil and Satan, who deceives the whole world; he was thrown down to the earth, and his angels were thrown down with him. Then I heard a loud

voice in heaven, saying, "Now the salvation, and the power, and the kingdom of our God and the authority of His Christ have come, for the accuser of our brethren has been thrown down, he who accuses them before our God day and night. And they overcame him because of the blood of the Lamb and because of the word of their testimony, and they did not love their life even when faced with death. For this reason, rejoice, O heavens and you who dwell in them. Woe to the earth and the sea, because the devil has come down to you, having great wrath, knowing that he has only a short time." (Rev. 12:7–12)

When Satan is cast out of heaven and down to earth, we are told he knows his time is short. He hates man. God brought Adam on the scene to correct the sin caused by Satan's disobedience. Satan knew he was an enemy, tempted him and Eve and won them over. Now he is out to wipe out their descendants, the human race. God brought the "last Adam" Jesus on the scene, and Satan tempted him without success. Jesus has been promised that He will rule over the descendants of Abraham, on the throne of David. There is left only one way that Satan can now defeat the purposes of God. That is that Jesus as king has no one to reign over, and throughout history Satan has made every attempt possible to wipe out all Israelites. Knowing his time is short Satan will make one final effort to end the human race, with a special effort to snuff out Israel. Only one thing will prevent Satan's success. He is not in control! God alone is in control, and He will allow Satan only to go so far. He will cut the days of Satan's evil short. "Unless those days had been cut short, no life would have been saved; but for the sake of the elect those days will be cut short" (Matt. 24:22).

God will allow Satan to have his flee, but really God is using all that happens to accomplish His purposes. Unbelievers are being separated as they follow Satan rather than God. Many are brought to their knees by this time of difficulty. We have seen earlier the multitude around the throne worshipping God in heaven. These were identified as those who had come out of the Great Tribulation. They had lost their lives for resisting Antichrist, but they were in heaven, and God said that they had won the victory (Rev. 7:9–15).

In chapter 13, we saw that one of the reasons God called the nation Israel was for them to carry the gospel to the nations. They did a very poor job of this, and even looked down upon Gentiles. When Israel's leaders called for the crucifixion of Messiah, they were set aside; and God begin using the Church to carry the gospel to others. God never gives up on what He purposes, and He still will hold Israel responsible to deliver His message to the world. The times of trouble during the tribulation period will result in Israel's obedience to go to the Nations. Probably those around the throne of God in Revelation chapter 7 are there as a result of Israelites carrying the message to the nations. Let us see who those are who carry God's message in the time of tribulation.

> After this I saw four angels standing at the four corners of the earth, holding back the four winds of the earth, so that no wind would blow on the earth or on the sea or on any tree. And I saw another angel ascending from the rising of the sun, having the seal of the living God; and he cried out with a loud voice to the our angels to whom it was granted to harm the earth and the sea, saying, "Do not harm the earth or the sea or the trees until we have sealed the bond-servants of our God on their foreheads." And I heard the number of those who were sealed, one hundred and forty-four thousand sealed from every tribe of the sons of Israel. (Rev. 7:1–4)

Those who are to be sealed are called God's bond-servants. They are sealed to be protected from the devastation that will fall upon the earth, and to do God's work. We surmise that God's work at this time is to get His message out in very difficult times. At the beginning of the seven-year period of tribulation there are no believers on the earth. All believers have been caught up to be with Christ (1 Thess. 4:13–18). Here we see 144,000 bond-servants sealed. What caused them to believe? God has His way of making things happen, and in this case it seems that He used two unique individuals.

> And I (God) will grant authority to my two witnesses, and they will prophesy for twelve hundred and sixty days, clothed in sackcloth." These are the two olive trees and the two lampstands that stand before the Lord of the earth. And if anyone wants to harm them, fire flows out of their mouth and devours their enemies; so if anyone wants to harm them, he must be killed in this way. These have the power to shut up the sky, so that rain will not fall during the days of their prophesying; and they have power over the waters to turn them into blood, and to strike the earth with every plague, as often as they desire. When they have finished their testimony, the beast that comes up out of the abyss will make war with them, and overcome them and kill them. And their dead bodies will lie in the street of the great city, which mystically is called Sodom and Egypt, where also their Lord was crucified. Those from the peoples and tribes and tongues and nations will look at their dead bodies for three and a half days, and will not permit their dead bodies to be laid in a tomb. And those who dwell on the earth will rejoice over them and celebrate; and they will send gifts to one another, because these two prophets tormented those who dwell on the earth. But after the three and a half days, the breath of life from God came into them, and they stood on their feet; and great fear fell upon those who were watching them. And they heard a loud voice from heaven saying to them, "Come up here." Then they went up into heaven in the cloud, and their ene-

mies watched them. And in that hour there was a great earthquake, and a tenth of the city fell; seven thousand people were killed in the earthquake, and the rest were terrified and gave glory to the God of heaven. (Rev. 11:3–13)

Something caused the 144,000 to turn to God and serve Him. Was it the Testimony of these two witnesses? Why else would God have what happened to these two, if it wasn't to get His message to the nations, and have Israel accomplish his calling for them to be witnesses to the nations. Jesus said, "This gospel of the kingdom shall be preached in the whole world as a testimony to all the nations, and then the end will come" (Matthew 24:14). Many believe the Church cannot be caught up to be with the Lord until the gospel in carried to all the world. But is that what this verse teaches? This verse says the gospel of "The Kingdom" must be carried to the whole world. Today are we proclaiming the Gospel of the Kingdom? Do we not preach the same gospel as the Apostle Paul? Paul tells us about the gospel he preached.

Now I make known to you, brethren, the gospel which I preached to you, which also you received, in which also you stand, by which also you are saved, if you hold fast the word which I preached to you, unless you believed in vain. For I delivered to you as of first importance what I also received, that Christ died for our sins according to the Scriptures, and that He was buried, and that He was raised on the third day according to the Scriptures. (1 Cor. 15:1–4)

The gospel Paul preached was the gospel of the death, burial, and resurrection of Jesus Christ. John the Baptist preached the "Gospel of the Kingdom. John was preaching a baptism of repentance for the forgiveness of sin for the Kingdom of Heaven was at hand.

The word of God came to John, the son of Zacharias, in the wilderness. And he came into all the district

> around the Jordan, preaching a baptism of repentance for the forgiveness of sins. (Luke 3:2b–3)

> Now in those days John the Baptist came, preaching in the wilderness of Judea, saying, "Repent, for the kingdom of heaven is at hand." (Matt. 3:1–2)

John the Baptist could preach this way, for Jesus was on earth at that time and was approaching the scene where john was baptizing. The 144,000 will be preaching the same "Gospel of the Kingdom," for at that time Jesus is about to return to earth at His second advent. This is the time that the gospel will be preached to the whole world (Matt. 24:14). The 144,000 will be obedient to God's call and carry the gospel to the nations, thus accomplishing God's purpose for Israel to carry His message to the entire world.

As we saw in Daniel, Satan's prince will cause great desolation; but in the end, destruction will be poured out on this desolator. How does this happen? Only with the return of the King of Kings.

THE KING OF KINGS ARRIVES CHAP. 15

The Lord Jesus arrived at the exact time in God's plan to provide redemption for mankind, remove the enmity between God and Man, and make it possible for men and women to have a relationship with God as their Father.

> But when the fullness of the time came, God sent forth His Son, born of a woman, born under the Law, that He might redeem those who were under the Law, that we might receive the adoption as sons. Because you are sons, God has sent forth the Spirit of His Son into our hearts, crying, "Abba! Father!" Therefore you are no longer a slave, but a son; and if a son, then an heir through God. (Gal. 4:4–7)

> But now in Christ Jesus you who formerly were far off have been brought near by the blood of Christ. For He Himself is our peace, who made both groups into one and broke down the barrier of the dividing wall, by abolishing in His flesh the enmity, which is the Law of commandments contained in ordinances, so that in Himself, He might make the two into one new man, thus establishing

peace, and might reconcile them both in one body to God through the cross, by it having put to death the enmity. (Eph. 2:13–16)

The Lord's second advent into human history will be no different. He will burst on the scene to stop the tragedies inflicted on humanity by Satan and his Antichrist and stop their efforts to annihilate the human race.

> And I saw heaven opened, and behold, a white horse, and He who sat on it is called Faithful and True, and in righteousness, He judges and wages war. His eyes are a flame of fire, and on His head are many diadems; and He has a name written on Him which no one knows except Himself. He is clothed with a robe dipped in blood, and His name is called The Word of God. And the armies, which are in heaven, clothed in fine linen, white and clean, were following Him on white horses. From His mouth comes a sharp sword, so that with it He may strike down the nations, and He will rule them with a rod of iron; and He treads the wine press of the fierce wrath of God, the Almighty. And on His robe and on His thigh He has a name written, "KING OF KINGS, AND LORD OF LORDS." (Rev. 19:11–16)

At Christ's first advent, many were looking for a King. They tried to replace the cross with a crown, and many failed to understand God's purpose. At his second coming, He will be wearing a crown, and ready to set things right and fulfill God's purposes. At Christ's second advent. the six things Daniel said would have to happen before God was finished with Daniel's people and the kingdom they desired would be established; will be accomplished. These six things were already noted in chapter 11, but we will repeat them again.

> Transgression will be finished.
> Sin will have ended.

Atonement will have been made for iniquity.
Everlasting righteousness will have been brought in.
Vision and prophecy will be sealed.
The most holy will be anointed.

What are the actions the Lord Jesus takes as King to accomplish these sinless and righteous conditions. In three moves He removes all opposition. First He eliminates the two ringleaders, the Antichrist and his false prophet.

> And the beast was seized, and with him the false prophet who performed the signs in his presence, by which he deceived those who had received the mark of the beast and those who worshiped his image; these two were thrown alive into the lake of fire which burns with brimstone. (Rev. 19:20)

It seems that as the end of the seven-year period of tribulation was approaching, that Satan could see his power slipping, and he uses sorcery and demons to assemble the nations against God at Jerusalem.

> And I saw coming out of the mouth of the dragon and out of the mouth of the beast and out of the mouth of the false prophet, three unclean spirits like frogs; for they are spirits of demons, performing signs, which go out to the kings of the whole world, to gather them together for the war of the great day of God, the Almighty. (Rev. 16:13–14)

The Lord's second step to remove opposition will be to eliminate those aligned with Antichrist.

> And the rest were killed with the sword, which came from the mouth of Him who sat on the horse, and all the birds were filled with their flesh. (Rev. 19:21)

After winning the battle over Satan's forces of evil, the Lord will send His angels to separate believers and unbelievers across the world.

> "But when the Son of Man comes in His glory, and all the angels with Him, then He will sit on His glorious throne. All the nations will be gathered before Him; and He will separate them from one another, as the shepherd separates the sheep from the goats; and He will put the sheep on His right, and the goats on the left. "Then the King will say to those on His right, 'Come, you who are blessed of My Father, inherit the kingdom prepared for you from the foundation of the world.... "Then He will also say to those on His left, 'Depart from Me, accursed ones, into the eternal fire which has been prepared for the Devil and his angels.... These will go away into eternal punishment, but the righteous into eternal life." (Matt. 25:31–34, 41, 46)

Now we need to consider a passage that is often misunderstood, that will help us understand what is happening at this time.

> "But of that day and hour no one knows, not even the angels of heaven, nor the Son, but the Father alone. For the coming of the Son of Man will be just like the days of Noah. For as in those days before the flood they were eating and drinking, marrying and giving in marriage, until the day that Noah entered the ark, and they did not understand until the flood came and took them all away; so will the coming of the Son of Man be. Then there will be two men in the field; one will be taken and one will be left. Two women will be grinding at the mill; one will be taken and one will be left. (Matt. 24:36–41)

The man and woman taken are often thought to be those taken to be with the Lord. That is not the case. These are those taken for judgment as the Lord makes ready for His kingdom, and is removing evil and unbelievers. The man and women left are believers, who the Lord leaves on earth to enter His Kingdom as He starts His reign.

At this point a little aside to help us better understand the comparison of the days of Noah with the day prior to the Lord's second advent to earth. My rendering of the passage in Matthew 24:

> For as in those days before the flood they were eating and drinking, marrying and giving in marriage, until the day that Noah entered the ark, and they did not understand until the flood came and took them all away; so will the coming of the Son of Man be. [Prior to the Lord's coming they will be eating and drinking (waiting in line for lattes), marrying and giving in marriage; stalled in stop and go traffic as they approach a sporting event, so they can cheer wildly, like there is no tomorrow, until the Lord returns, and they did not realize He was coming.] (Matt. 24:38–39)

God, the Father, has promised the Lord Jesus the nations (Ps. 2). He is to be sovereign King over them. Satan has been a pretender trying to have power. It is impossible to have two sovereigns, especially when their agendas are different. This is even more true when the rightful sovereign is seeking to bring in a righteous realm, which the pretender is trying to destroy; thus the Lord third and last step is to bind Satan and eliminate his evil influence from the world.

> Then I saw an angel coming down from heaven, holding the key of the abyss and a great chain in his hand. And he laid hold of the dragon, the serpent of old, who is the devil and Satan, and bound him for a thousand years; and he threw him into the abyss, and shut it and sealed it over him, so that he would not deceive the nations any longer, until the thousand years were completed; after these things he must be released for a short time. (Rev. 20:1–3)

For accomplishing the work of salvation God, the Father, promised Christ the nations.

> "I will surely tell of the decree of the Lord: He said to Me, 'You are My Son, Today I have begotten You. 'Ask of Me, and I will surely give the nations as Your inheritance, and the very ends of the earth as Your possession. 'You shall break them with a rod of iron, You shall shatter them like earthenware.'" (Ps. 2:7–9)

The Lord has long desired that those promised to Him, would be with Him as seen in His prayer on the night he was betrayed.

> But now I come to You; and these things I speak in the world so that they may have My joy made full in themselves. I have given them Your word; and the world has hated them, because they are not of the world, even as I am not of the world. I do not ask You to take them out of the world, but to keep them from the evil one. They are not of the world, even as I am not of the world. Sanctify them in the truth; Your word is truth. As You sent Me into the world, I also have sent them into the world. For their sakes I sanctify Myself, that they themselves also may be sanctified in truth. "I do not ask on behalf of these alone, but for those also who believe in Me through their word; that they may all be one; even as You, Father, are in Me and I in You, that they also may be in Us, so that the world may believe that You sent Me. The glory which You have given Me I have given to them, that they may be one, just as We are one; I in them and You in Me, that they may be perfected in unity, so that the world may know that You sent Me, and loved them, even as You have loved Me. Father, I desire that they also, whom You have given Me,

be with Me where I am, so that they may see My glory which You have given Me, for You loved Me before the foundation of the world. "O righteous Father, although the world has not known You, yet I have known You; and these have known that You sent Me; and I have made Your name known to them, and will make it known, so that the love with which You loved Me may be in them, and I in them." (John 17:13–26)

Now the Lord will gather up those He has longed to be with, and have them see His glory.

"But immediately after the tribulation of those days the sun will be darkened, and the moon will not give its light, and the stars will fall from the sky, and the powers of the heavens will be shaken. And then the sign of the Son of Man will appear in the sky, and then all the tribes of the earth will mourn, and they will see the Son of Man coming on the clouds of the sky with power and great glory. And He will send forth His angels with a great trumpet and they will gather together His elect from the four winds, from one end of the sky to the other. (Matt. 24:29–31)

In His coming, Christ will remove evil and opposition to God, He will gather up those who are His to be with Him forever, but He has also upheld the integrity of His Father. Throughout time God has made promises to individuals, which Satan attempted to keep from being fulfilled. God promised Abraham a land forever. Christ is now ready to rule over that land and protect it from evil forever. God promised David that one of his descendants would rule on his throne forever. Jesus is now ready to take his seat on that throne. Scripture tells us He will reign on this earth 1000 years (Rev. 20:4–6), during which time all the Old Testament promised will be fulfilled. After that He will reign forever in the heavenly New Jerusalem on the new earth. In spite of what men say, you can take God's promises to the bank; Jesus is ready to see them fulfilled.

Many say God's promises are being fulfilled by Jesus sitting at the Father's right hand on God's throne in heaven. A problem with this view is that the promises made to Abraham, David and many others had to do with the physical earth they stood on and that we today still stand on. In order that the promises made by God to men through the ages be fulfilled as promised, it is necessary that Christ reign on this earth.

With Adam God had a purpose for man, and that purpose for man will happen, because of the work of "The Last Adam," the Lord Jesus Christ. Not only has Jesus desired that we be with Him and see His glory, but He is going to share all that the Father has promised him. We also will share in God's purposes for man. As King Jesus is going to reign, but He is going to share that reign with those who are His.

> Then I saw thrones, and they sat on them, and judgment was given to them. And I saw the souls of those who had been beheaded because of their testimony of Jesus and because of the word of God, and those who had not worshiped the beast or his image, and had not received the mark on their forehead and on their hand; and they came to life and reigned with Christ for a thousand years. The rest of the dead did not come to life until the thousand years were completed. This is the first resurrection. Blessed and holy is the one who has a part in the first resurrection; over these the second death has no power, but they will be priests of God and of Christ and will reign with Him for a thousand years. (Rev. 20:4–6)

The Apostle Paul saw all believers as being "In Christ." In this position, we share many privileges with our Savior.

As seen above, we will reign with Him.

1. God the Father loves us as He loved Christ; "You loved them, even as You have loved Me." (John 17:23b)
2. We share heavenly blessings; "Blessed be the God and Father of our Lord Jesus Christ, who has blessed us with every spiritual blessing in the heavenly places in Christ." (Eph. 1:3)
3. We have been adopted into God's family as sons, "He predestined us to adoption as sons through Jesus Christ to Himself, according to the kind intention of His will." (Eph. 1:5)
4. Jesus calls us His brothers and sisters, "For both he that sanctifieth and they who are sanctified are all of one: for which cause he is not ashamed to call them brethren." (Heb. 2:11)
5. We will be heirs with Christ, "And if children, heirs also, heirs of God and fellow heirs with Christ, if indeed we suffer with Him so that we may also be glorified with Him." (Rom. 8:17). Fellow heirs speak of equality. What a generous Savior is ours!

To better understand Christ's kingdom reign, let's do some review. Let's look back to the beginning of the seven-year tribulation. At that time there were only unbelievers on the earth. All believers had been caught up to be with the Lord (1 Thess. 4:13–18). We saw that shortly there were those who resisted the Antichrist became believers and carried the gospel to the world, resulting in a great revival.

At Christ's Second Advent sin and sinners will be removed from the earth, and the Kingdom age will begin with only believers on the earth, "But the one who endures to the end, he will be saved" (Matt. 24:13). Many would take "saved" here to mean salvation, if you hang in there and live a good life you will be saved. This is not what is meant. This verse is dealing with the time of the tribulation. What is meant is that those who are able to live through the tribulation will be delivered from Satan's brutalities and allowed to enter Christ's kingdom.

During the Kingdom Age Christ will bring to fulfillment all the promises that God made to the Old Testament saints. As seen above these promises were made concerning the earth those receiving the promises lived on. Thus for Christ to make a true fulfillment for these promises He will need to reign on the earth, the same one they lived on and carry out everything that was promised. In particular the Lord will fulfill God's promises to Abraham concerning his descendants. Israel has been rebellious, but God has promised to gather them back to Himself.

> "For a brief moment I forsook you, but with great compassion I will gather you. In an outburst of anger, I hid My face from you for a moment, but with everlasting loving kindness I will have compassion on you," Says the Lord your Redeemer. (Isa. 54:7–8)

Yes, God will keep His promises, in no way will He allow ill repute to come against His name. Israelites have been hated among the nations, which resulted in the nations also having lost respect for Israel's God. God will restore his respect among the nations by cleaning up Israel.

> "Therefore say to the house of Israel, 'Thus says the Lord God, "It is not for your sake, O house of Israel, that I am about to act, but for My holy name, which you have profaned among the nations where you went. I will vindicate the holiness of My great name which has been profaned among the nations, which you have profaned in their midst. Then the nations will know that I am the Lord," declares the Lord God, "when I prove Myself holy among you in their sight. For I will take you from the nations, gather you from all the lands and bring you into your own land. Then I will sprinkle clean water on you, and you will be clean; I will cleanse you from all your filthiness and from all your idols. Moreover, I will give you a new heart and put a new spirit within you; and I will remove the heart of stone from your flesh and give you a heart of flesh. I will put My Spirit within you and cause you to walk in My statutes, and you will be careful

to observe My ordinances. You will live in the land that I gave to your forefathers; so you will be My people, and I will be your God. Moreover, I will save you from all your uncleanness; and I will call for the grain and multiply it, and I will not bring a famine on you. I will multiply the fruit of the tree and the produce of the field, so that you will not receive again the disgrace of famine among the nations. Then you will remember your evil ways and your deeds that were not good, and you will loathe yourselves in your own sight for your iniquities and your abominations. I am not doing this for your sake," declares the Lord God, "let it be known to you. Be ashamed and confounded for your ways, O house of Israel!" Thus says the Lord GOD; "On the day that I cleanse you from all your iniquities, I will cause the cities to be inhabited, and the waste places will be rebuilt. The desolate land will be cultivated instead of being desolation in the sight of everyone who passes by. They will say, 'This desolate land has become like the Garden of Eden; and the waste, desolate and ruined cities are fortified and inhabited.' Then the nations that are left round about you will know that I, the Lord, have rebuilt the ruined places and planted that which was desolate; I, the Lord, have spoken and will do it." Thus says the Lord God, "This also I will let the house of Israel ask Me to do for them: I will increase their men like a flock. Like the flock for sacrifices, like the flock at Jerusalem during her appointed feasts, so will the waste cities be filled with flocks of men. Then they will know that I am the Lord."" (Ezek. 36:22–38)

God's original plan for Israel included them being a blessing to the nations. Through Israel the Savior would be born with salvation for all nations. Israel was to carry the message of salvation to the nations.

Obedience would bring God's physical blessings upon the nation Israel. We see that happen during the reign of King David and the early days of Solomon's reign. When Israel turned away from God in disobedience, Israel was brought down to ruin and captivity. At the end of the tribulation period when Israel realizes the one who was pierced/Jesus (Zech. 12:10) was truly their Messiah, Israel as a nation will begin to fulfill God's purposes for them, as Ezekiel's above prophesy predicted. Only believers will enter the beginning of the Kingdom Age, and with Christ reigning, things on earth will no longer be in conflict with God's purposes. God, Himself says at this time He also will have reason to rejoice, with the result He will bring physical blessing upon Israel as a nation.

> "I will also rejoice in Jerusalem and be glad in My people; and there will no longer be heard in her the voice of weeping and the sound of crying. "No longer will there be in it an infant who lives but a few days, Or an old man who does not live out his days; For the youth will die at the age of one hundred And the one who does not reach the age of one hundred will be thought accursed. "They will build houses and inhabit them; they will also plant vineyards and eat their fruit. They will not build and another inhabit, They will not plant and another eat; for as the lifetime of a tree, so will be the days of My people, and My chosen ones will wear out the work of their hands. They will not labor in vain, Or bear children for calamity; For they are the offspring of those blessed by the Lord, And their descendants with them. It will also come to pass that before they call, I will answer; and while they are still speaking, I will hear. The wolf and the lamb will graze together, and the lion will eat straw like the ox; and dust will be the serpent's food. They will do no evil or harm in all My holy mountain," says the Lord. (Isa. 65:19–25)

When Christ reigns as King, we have seen that Israelites will be living in obedience, and God will rejoice and bless Israel. The land will blossom in fruitfulness. One of God's early commands for man was to fruitful and multiply. The population of the earth depleted during the tribulation period will be replenished as a result of the perfect conditions on the earth during Christ's reign. Above we saw Ezekiel prophesy that God would increase men like a flock. Israel said that there would no longer be an infant, who lives but a few days.

We have seen that those who live through the tribulation and enter the Kingdom Age will all be believers. Although everyone at the beginning of the Kingdom are believers they are still in fleshly, earthly bodies tainted by sin and the curse. Being obedient believers they will be quick to fulfill one of God's first command, "be fruitful and multiply." This being the case, and it still being true that God has no grandchildren, all the children born will need to come to faith in Christ, and be born again.

One might ask, "Won't it be a little scary to live at this time, after all Christ is ruling with an iron rod."

> And He shall rule them with a rod of iron, as the vessel of the potter are broken to pieces. (Rev. 2:27)

> And she gave birth to a son, a male child, who is to rule all the nations with a rod of iron; and her child was caught up to God and to His throne. (Rev. 12:5)

To those who think one ruling with a rod of iron is scary, we can say, "It is only scary for the disobedient. A benevolent ruler, who maintains justice, will provide safety and comfort for His people. Those who live in obedience and honor their King will have no fear. How different from most times in the earth's history when a majority of earth's population has lived in fear. Truly, it will be during the Kingdom Age that we will see human government operate as God intended, to protect the person who does good.

> For rulers are not a cause of fear for good behavior, but for evil. Do you want to have no fear of author-

ity? Do what is good and you will have praise from the same; for it/government is a minister of God to you for good. But if you do what is evil, be afraid, for it does not bear the sword for nothing, for it is a minister of God, an avenger who brings wrath on the one who practices evil. (Rom. 13:3–4)

The Psalmist understood the use of the rod better than most. "Even though I walk through the valley of the shadow of death, I fear no evil, for You are with me; Your rod and Your staff, they comfort me" (Ps. 23:4).

At this point we may ask, "Where do we as believers today fit into this picture?" We have been told we will rule and reign with Christ, and be co-heirs with him; however, before Christ comes back to earth to reign, believers will have been caught up to be with Him in heaven (1 Thess. 4:13–18). At the time we are caught up to be with Him we also will receive resurrection bodies. How do we know this?

Let's look what the Bible says about resurrection.

But now Christ has been raised from the dead, the first fruits of those who are asleep. For since by a man came death, by a man also came the resurrection of the dead. For as in Adam all die, so also in Christ all will be made alive. But each in his own order: Christ the first fruits, after that those who are Christ's at His coming, (1 Cor. 15:20–23)

First we see that Christ is the first fruits of the resurrection. When a farmer or an orchardist sees the first fruit from his labors, he knows there will be a crop to follow. The same is tell with resurrection, since Jesus is said to be the first fruits, we can be assured that there will follow the resurrection of many others. This passage also tells us there will be an order in resurrections. All resurrections will not occur at the same time. Those who are the next to be resurrected are said to be those who are His at His coming. Believers of this age are said to be the Lord's, and He said on the night He was betrayed He desired for them to be with Him.

> I (Jesus) have manifested Your name to the men whom You gave Me out of the world; they were Yours and You gave them to Me, and they have kept Your word. Now they have come to know that everything You have given Me is from You; for the words which You gave Me I have given to them; and they received them and truly understood that I came forth from You, and they believed that You sent Me. I ask on their behalf; I do not ask on behalf of the world, but of those whom You have given Me; for they are Yours; and all things that are Mine are Yours, and Yours are Mine; and I have been glorified no longer in the world; and yet they themselves are in the world, and I come to You. Holy Father, keep them in Your name, the name which You have given Me, that they may be one even as We are. While I was with them, I was keeping them in Your name which You have given Me; and I guarded them and not one of them perished but the son of perdition, so that the Scripture would be fulfilled. (John 17:6–12)

> The glory which You have given Me I have given to them, that they may be one, just as We are one; I in them and You in Me, that they may be perfected in unity, so that the world may know that You sent Me, and loved them, even as You have loved Me. Father, I desire that they also, whom You have given Me, be with Me where I am, so that they may see My glory which You have given Me, for You loved Me before the foundation of the world. (John 17:22–24)

Jesus has long desires that those the Father has given Him should be with Him. We have seen earlier that there is a time coming when He will come to gather them up to meet him in the clouds (1 Thess. 4:13–18). It is at that time at His coming that we are told the next order of resurrection will occur. We who are His will meet Him in the air and be changed. These old bodies, that are filled with pain, will be transformed into resurrected bodies.

> Now I say this, brethren, that flesh and blood cannot inherit the kingdom of God; nor does the perishable inherit the imperishable. Behold, I tell you a mystery; we will not all sleep, but we will all be changed, in a moment, in the twinkling of an eye, at the last trumpet; for the trumpet will sound, and the dead will be raised imperishable, and we will be changed. For this perishable must put on the imperishable, and this mortal must put on immortality. But when this perishable will have put on the imperishable, and this mortal will have put on immortality, then will come about the saying that is written, "Death is swallowed up in victory. (1 Cor. 15:50–54)

From these scriptures we see that believers of this age will be caught up to be with the Lord before the tribulation period and at that time they will receive resurrection bodies. Believers who live through the tribulation period will enter the Kingdom Age with physical mortal bodies. During the Kingdom Age they will be fruitful and multiply, and repopulate the earth. It has been said the Bible tells us what we need to know, but not always all we would like to know. This is one of those situations, and leaves us with a question. How can people with mortal physical bodies and others with resurrection bodies be on the earth at the same time?

Let's consider what we do know. Christ's relation with the church is compared to marriage, and in Revelation we see the Marriage of the Lamb, which speaks of Christ's bride. The bride is said to be clothed in fine linen, which is the righteous acts of the saints, thus equating the Bride with Saints. At this time the church has already been caught up to be with Christ in Heaven; thus the bride here must be the Church, the Body of Christ, united with Christ in marriage in an eternal relationship.

> But as the church is subject to Christ, so also the wives ought to be to their husbands in everything. Husbands, love your wives, just as Christ also loved the church and gave Himself up for her, so that He might sanctify her, having cleansed her by the washing of water with the word, that He might present to Himself the church in all her glory, having no spot or wrinkle or any such thing; but that she would be holy and blameless. So husbands ought also to love their own wives as their own bodies. He who loves his own wife loves himself; for no one ever hated his own flesh, but nourishes and cherishes it, just as Christ also does the church, because we are members of His body. (Eph. 5:24–29)

> Let us rejoice and be glad and give the glory to Him, for the marriage of the Lamb has come and His bride has made herself ready." It was given to her to clothe herself in fine linen, bright and clean; for the fine linen is the righteous acts of the Saints. (Rev. 19:7–8)

The ending phrase of the above scripture, "fine linen is the righteous acts of the Saints," needs some explaining, which will add to our understanding. The fine linen the bride is adorned in is said to be the righteous acts of the Saints. After one becomes a believer, he or she is called to radiate the character of their new heavenly Father.

> But God, being rich in mercy, because of His great love with which He loved us, even when we were dead in our transgressions, made us alive together with Christ by grace you have been saved, and raised us up with Him, and seated us with Him in

the heavenly places in Christ Jesus, so that in the ages to come He might show the surpassing riches of His grace in kindness toward us in Christ Jesus. For by grace you have been saved through faith; and that not of yourselves, it is the gift of God; not as a result of works, so that no one may boast. For we are His workmanship, created in Christ Jesus for good works, which God prepared beforehand so that we would walk in them. (Eph. 2:4–10)

When one becomes a Christian, God works through that person to show forth His grace and kindness, and such a person becomes the workmanship of God. As we serve God and allow Him to work through us, scripture tells us there will be eternal rewards. It seems that the righteous acts that result in the fine linen, Saints will wear at "The Wedding Supper of the Lamb" are part of these rewards.

Be glad in that day and leap for joy, for behold, your reward is great in heaven. (Luke 6:23a)

Now he who plants and he who waters are one; but each will receive his own reward according to his own labor. (1 Cor. 3:8)

"Behold, I am coming quickly, and My reward is with Me, to render to every man according to what he has done. (Rev. 22:12)

The Apostle Paul tells us we must all appear before the judgment seat of Christ, "For we must all appear before the judgment seat of Christ, so that each one may be recompensed for his deeds in the body, according to what he has done, whether good or bad (2 Cor. 5:10). This judgment is for our deeds as believers, for good deeds in our service for the Lord will be rewarded. This leaves us with the question, "When does this judgment happen?" Since it is before the Lord. This judgment has to be after we are caught up to be with the Lord. If the fine linen worn by Saints at "The Wedding Supper of the Lamb" is a result of righteous acts of the Saints, then this judgment would have to be before "The Wedding supper of the Lamb." This leads us to believe this event will occur in heaven while the tribulation is occurring on the earth. The armies of heaven, which return to earth with the Lord at His second advent, are hardly wearing gear for warfare. They are wearing fine linen, which would cause us to believe these are the same Saints, who are united with the Lord at the wedding, and the Judgment Seat of Christ would have to precede "The Marriage Supper of the Lamb." This would cause us to conclude "the Wedding supper of the Lamb" also occurs in heaven, while the tribulation is occurring on earth.

> And I saw heaven opened, and behold, a white horse, and He who sat on it is called Faithful and True, and in righteousness He judges and wages war. His eyes are a flame of fire, and on His head are many diadems; and He has a name written on Him, which no one knows except Himself. He is clothed with a robe dipped in blood, and His name is called The Word of God. And the armies, which are in heaven, clothed in fine linen, white and clean, were following Him on white horses. From His mouth comes a sharp sword, so that with it He may strike down the nations, and He will rule them with a rod of iron; and He treads the wine press of the fierce wrath of God, the Almighty. And on His robe and on His thigh He has a name written, "KING OF KINGS, AND LORD OF LORDS. (Rev. 19:11–16)

We thus conclude that during the Lord's reign there will be both mortal people on earth, and also those in resurrection bodies. The Lord did not chose to reveal to us how these two groups will relate to each other, then that those who return with Christ will rule with Him. What God does allow us to see is that, when it comes time to straighten things out on the earth and remove evil, Jesus can handle it. The armies of heaven return with Christ to see Him win the battle, without them raising a hand. Christ strikes down the nations with a sharp sword out of His mouth. It seems all the nations who are wrapped up in evil efforts at our Lord's return, cannot withstand a word from His mouth. Do you feel safe and secure? Standing with Christ you are on the victorious side. Those who return with Christ will see their King win the victory, and they will be there to share His long reign. Share His reign only because of the victories He has won, and because He wants to graciously share His reign with them.

> "Blessed and holy is the one who has a part in the first resurrection; over these the second death has no power, but they will be priests of God and of Christ and will reign with Him for a thousand years (Rev. 20:6).

At this time, the earth will flourish with fruitfulness. God's honor will be upheld, as all His promises to the Saints throughout the ages will be fulfilled, as Jesus reigns as King.

> But now Christ has been raised from the dead, the first fruits of those who are asleep. For since by a man came death, by a man also came the resurrection of the dead. For as in Adam all die, so also in Christ all will be made alive. But each in his own order: Christ the first fruits, after that those the God and Father, when He has abolished all rule and all authority and power. For He must reign until He has put all His enemies under His feet. The last enemy that will be abolished is death. For He/God the Father has put all things in subjection under His/Jesus's feet. But when He says, "All things are put in subjection," it is evident that He is excepted who put all things in subjection to Him. When all things are subjected to Him, then the Son Himself also will be subjected to the One who subjected all things to Him, so that God may be all in all. (1 Cor. 15:20–28)

After Jesus has put all opposition under His feet, God will again be all in all. This One who is King of Kings is none other than our

Savior. Even the Apostle Paul could not put into words what is in store for us.

> Thanks be to God for His indescribable gift! (2 Cor. 9:15)

> Oh, the depth of the riches both of the wisdom and knowledge of God! How unsearchable are His judgments and unfathomable His ways! (Rom. 11:33)

THE SPIRITUAL WAR END   CHAP.16

At Christ's second advent, we saw Him beginning to deal with sin and unbelief. He defeated the forces that Satan had gathered from among the nations with the sharp sword from His mouth, "From His mouth comes a sharp sword, so that with it He may strike down the nations, and He will rule them with a rod of iron (Rev. 19:5a). Next the Beast and False Prophet were taken and cast into "The Lake of Fire" (Rev. 19:20). After which all the rest of those opposing Him were killed with the sword that came out of His mouth. With these actions the Lord prepared for the believers, who had come through the tribulation period alive to enter His Kingdom. The last act of the Lord for preparation to begin His Kingdom reign was to remove the presence of Satan's evil. This He did by having Satan bound and confined to the abyss.

> Then I saw an angel coming down from heaven, holding the key of the abyss and a great chain in his hand. And he laid hold of the dragon, the serpent of old, who is the devil and Satan, and bound him for a thousand years; and he threw him into the abyss, and shut it and sealed it over him, so that he would not deceive the nations any longer, until the

thousand years were completed; after these things,
he must be released for a short time. (Rev. 20:1–3)

We might ask, "Why didn't the Lord have Satan thrown into the Lake of Fire, like the Beast and False Prophet?" This will take some explaining, but the final answer is the Lord is not finished using Satan to accomplish His purposes. That may sound like a strange statement, but it has always been true. Satan has set out to be like "The Most High," but He has never been able to do anything that the Lord did not allow. Now let's look into how the Lord will use Satan for the last time.

We have seen that at the beginning of the tribulation period, there were only unbelievers left on the earth, and at the beginning of the Kingdom Age there will be only believers left on the earth. These individuals will have lived through the Tribulation, and being believers they were not killed with the unbelievers of the nations, or gathered up by the angels for judgment. However, even though they are believers, they are still in fleshly, mortal, earthly bodies tainted by sin and the curse. Being obedient believers they will be quick to fulfill one of God's first command, "be fruitful and multiply." This being the case, and it is still true that God has no grandchildren, everyone born during the Kingdom Age will need to experience the new birth. Children born during the kingdom age to mortal parents will still be victims of original sin passed from father to child from the days of Adam. To become children of God, they must be born again by placing their faith in Christ for redemption from sin. It would seem that belief in Christ as Savior would be an easy choice at this time, since He is ruling as a benevolent King with everything on earth seeming set in order. Although life and condition are good during the Kingdom Age, not all will turn to Christ in belief. Because of the old nature passed on from the fall of Adam and Eve, there will always be those who buck against any restraint even when times are good. Christ will rule with a rod of iron during the Kingdom Age, and sudden justice will prevail, so few will openly resist ordered society, for fear of falling into judgment. However, many will harbor rebellion in their hearts against the rules of Christ's government, and will only give lip service to His rule.

In order to separate true belief from lip service, God will use Satan once again at the end of this earth's history to cause the necessary division. This is why as we read above he must be released for a short time. When Satan is released and there is someone else to follow rather than Christ, all those who would only give lip service to Christ's rule will flock to Satan.

> When the thousand years are completed, Satan will be released from his prison, and will come out to deceive the nations which are in the four corners of the earth, Gog and Magog, to gather them together for the war; the number of them is like the sand of the seashore. And they came up on the broad plain of the earth and surrounded the camp of the saints and the beloved city, and fire came down from heaven and devoured them. And the devil who deceived them was thrown into the lake of fire and brimstone, where the beast and the false prophet are also; and they will be tormented day and night forever and ever. (Rev. 20:7–10)

There must be many lessons for us to learn at this point. We see that after a thousand years of imprisonment, Satan has no change of heart. At his release, he mobilizes all who will follow him against God. The numbers who turn to him are amazing. Man can make many excuses for not following God, but all are without substance. During the Kingdom Age conditions will reach the point of Utopia, all that man could ever want will be available. But there is one problem, man will not want to give allegiance to another, man will want to be his own god, and when opportunity comes he will turn from Jesus, "The True God." No excuse is justified for turning from God, and pride will keep one from enjoying all that God has for those who turn to His Son for Salvation.

Satan with all his power and deceptive ability is only a pond in God's hands. At the end of the Kingdom Age, when he is released, he is able to mobilize all the forces of unbelief. He leads them against the Beloved City, Jerusalem, the Capital of Christ's Kingdom. Again he attempts to rid the earth of Christ and the rule of God. Think this is scary? Not at all. in an instant fire comes turn from heaven and wipes out the entire force that Satan has been able to mobilize. Yes, God wants to use all those who He has created, and He will use them. He even will use Satan to separate true believer from those who live in opposition to God's purposes. All will be used, but only those who serve willingly will be rewarded. Everyone has a choice, what will you chose? At this point God is finishing using Satan, and he does go to his final reward. His reward is to join his two co-hearts of earlier times.

> And the devil who deceived them was thrown into the lake of fire and brimstone, where the beast and the false prophet are also; and they will be tormented day and night forever and ever. (Rev. 20:10)

There is a lesson here also concerning eternal punishment. When Satan is cast into the Lake of fire, he joins the Breast and the False Prophet. They have been there for 1000 years and they are still there. The verse goes on to say, "They will be tormented day and night forever and ever." There are those who say a loving God would not punish any-one eternally. However, that is not what the scriptures say! The personal beings, angels and humans, were created by God to be in a relationship with Him forever, but they were also given a free will. They can chose to not have a relationship with God, but it is impossible for them to choose not to exist. It is their choice, will they have a forever relation-ship with God, or chose to have nothing to do with God. They said, "We want to be our own boss, God we want nothing to do with you." All God said was, "Have it your own way." Sad thing is, that for one to separate himself from God, that person also separates himself from all that is good.

At this point, with Satan cast permanently into the Lake of Fire and all those who followed him destroyed, all opposition to God sover-eignty is removed. God being holy must deal with sin; however, He is a just God. Because of this He will give everyone his or her day in court. This will occur immediately after the removal of Satan.

> Then I saw a great white throne and Him who sat upon it, from whose presence earth and heaven fled

> away, and no place was found for them. And I saw
> the dead, the great and the small, standing before
> the throne, and books were opened; and another
> book was opened, which is the book of life; and the
> dead were judged from the things, which were writ-
> ten in the books, according to their deeds. And the
> sea gave up the dead, which were in it, and death
> and Hades gave up the dead, which were in them;
> and they were judged, every one of them according
> to their deeds. Then death and Hades were thrown
> into the lake of fire. This is the second death, the
> lake of fire. And if anyone's name was not found
> written in the book of life, he was thrown into the
> lake of fire. (Rev. 20:11–15)

It needs to be noted that these who are standing in judgment are judged for their deeds. These are those who would say, "I lived a good life." "I certainly didn't do the awful things he/she did." "I never killed anyone." And on and on go their comments. One thing these people didn't seem to consider is who sets the standards in this case. It is not ones neighbor or the other guy. God sets the standard, and His standard is perfection, God does not grade on the curve. We all fall short, one sin causes disqualification, and our righteousness counts for nothing.

> For all have sinned and fall short of the glory of
> God, (Rom. 3:23)

> For whoever keeps the whole law and yet stumbles
> in one point, he has become guilty of all. (James
> 2:10)

> For all of us have become like one who is unclean,
> and all our righteous deeds are like a filthy gar-
> ment/rags. (Isa. 64:6a)

Why is God so strict? Well, once God created a Paradise, it was called the "Garden of Eden." Then he placed man and woman in the garden with a free will. Their bad decision, not to obey God, brought sin into the garden, and it was no longer Paradise, and the whole earth was also rent with problems. God has promised a lot to those will receive and trust His Son. What God has promised will come to pass in another Paradise, the New Earth and New Heaven. God always keeps His promises; therefore, He will not allow one sin to come into the New Earth.

You ask, "What then is our hope?" We all have sinned and God will not allow one sin into heaven. We have covered this earlier, but it is so important we need to say it again. The wages of sin is death (Rom. 6:23). If we pay the price and die for ourselves, it would result in our being separated from God forever. Our only hope is a substitute to take our place, and God Himself, in the person of God the Son was willing to do that. He took our place, we should have been on the cross.

Let me include my personal experience. I spent the first 23 years of my life trying to determine how much good I needed to do in order to step over the line to where I was good enough for God's acceptance. Harvey, who led me to the Lord said, "Ron, you are trying to do what has already been done. Christ died in your place; you were the sinner, who should have been on the cross. He did it for you, now all you need to do is say Thank You!" That was the greatest statement I have ever heard, and my life has never been the same. No, getting to heaven is not a balancing act, as many think, where your good deed are weighed against bad deeds, and if good out-weighs the bad God will accept you.

We have a sinless Savior, who did not need to die for His own sins; and therefore, could die for us. He paid it all for us. He paid the wages of death for our sins, and imputed His righteousness to our account. If the believer were to look at his account in heaven; it would read, " Perfect Righteousness." He made Him who knew no sin to be sin on our behalf, so that we might become the righteousness of God in Him (2 Cor. 5:21). Yes, only the person with the Righteousness of Christ will be allowed into Heaven, the result being; Heaven will always be perfect.

Now let's get back to "The White Throne Judgment." We have seen that everyone there is standing on their deeds, and all these deeds do not add up to perfect righteousness. Everyone comes up short, because their names were not found in "The Book of Life." They stand on their own deeds, they had never accepted Christ's sacrifice for them, and thus their name had never been added to "The Book of Life." They were still in their sin, which disqualified them from entering heaven, for God will not allow heaven to be contaminated. He will keep it perfect for those who have become His children, by accepting His Son and the perfect righteousness He offers.

One more issue needs to be considered. Scripture says we will all stand before the Judgment Seat of Christ.

> But you, why do you judge your brother? Or you again, why do you regard your brother with contempt? For we will all stand before the judgment seat of God. (Rom. 14:10)

> For we must all appear before the judgment seat of Christ, so that each one may be recompensed for his deeds in the body, according to what he has done, whether good or bad. (2 Cor. 5:10)

Many interpret this to state that there is a day coming, when everyone will stand before Christ, and at that time they will find out if they are allowed into heaven. What these individuals do not understand is there are two different judgments. The "Judgment Seat of Christ" and "The Great white Throne Judgment," and they are not the same. In the two passages above Romans and 2 Corinthians, the Apostle Paul is speaking to believers. These passages have nothing to do with salvation, those Paul is addressing are saved. Paul is encouraging them to faithfully serve the Lord, who will reward them. These rewards will be determined at "The Judgment Seat of Christ."

"The Great White Throne Judgment" does concern salvation. Those standing before it are standing on their own deeds, their own merits. They say they are good enough and God should accept them, they have rejected the perfect righteousness Christ offers, that is necessary to enter heaven. They do not accept God's way, and as a result are separated from God forever, which is the "Lake of fire."

At this point, all opposition to God and His purposes have been removed. The Spiritual Warfare has been won. God's King is in place to rule. He had accomplished every purpose that God had for man. The Good News is our generous Savior is going to share with those the Father has given Him, what the Father has given Him. We will be co-heirs with Him and reign with Him forever. God again will be all in all.

> For He has put all things in subjection under His feet. But when He says, "All things are put in subjection," it is evident that He is excepted who (the Father) put all things in subjection to Him (Jesus). When all things are subjected to Him, then the Son Himself also will be subjected to the One who subjected all things to Him, so that God may be all in all. (1 Cor. 15:27–28)

All opposition will be gone, and God will have a family of sons and daughters, and together they will enjoy each other forever.

HOME AT LAST CHAP. 17

In the beginning, the omnipotent God spoke; and from His power, in an instant, our magnificent universe came into being. It is He who made the earth by His power, who established the world by His wisdom; and by His understanding, He has stretched out the heavens (Jer. 10:12). Peer into the night skies, watch the stars, or observe some of the pictures taken from space; and a person cannot help being spellbound.

God then decided to create an environment in which man could live. He took six days to accomplish this, and His efforts included the man and creatures to live in this environment. Oh, yes! The beautiful earth God created was tainted by sin, but still, its beauty and magnificence still causes us to gasp in open-mouthed wonder at its sites.

As the Lord was preparing His disciples for His soon-approaching departure from them, He asked them not to be troubled; for He was going to prepare a place for them wherein they could be together.

> "Do not let your heart be troubled; believe in God, believe also in Me. In My Father's house are many dwelling places; if it were not so, I would have told you; for I go to prepare a place for you. If I go and prepare a place for you, I will come again and

receive you to Myself, that where I am, there you may be also." (John 14:1–3)

He is preparing this place for all believers. Can you imagine what it will be like? He has been working on it for nearly two thousand years, and He was a skilled carpenter. Compare six days with two thousand years, and no words can explain what is in store for us. It will all be new. This beautiful earth will not due. In fact, the old earth and heavens was tainted by sin; and the curse could not stand before the Lord when He took His position at the "white throne of judgment."

> Then I saw a great white throne and Him who sat upon it, from whose presence earth and heaven fled away, and no place was found for them. (Rev. 20:11)

Yes, this earth and the heavens will pass. The Apostle Peter tells us more about its demise.

> Know this first of all, that in the last days mockers will come with their mocking, following after their own lusts, and saying, "Where is the promise of His coming? For ever since the fathers fell asleep, all continues just as it was from the beginning of creation." For when they maintain this, it escapes their notice that by the word of God the heavens existed long ago and the earth was formed out of water and by water, through which the world at that time was destroyed, being flooded with water. But by His word the present heavens and earth are being reserved for fire, kept for the Day of Judgment and destruction of ungodly men. But do not let this one fact escape your notice, beloved, that with the Lord one day is like a thousand years, and a thousand years like one day. The Lord is not slow about His promise, as some count slowness, but is patient toward you, not wishing for any to perish but for all to come to repentance. But the

> day of the Lord will come like a thief, in which the
> heavens will pass away with a roar and the elements
> will be destroyed with intense heat, and the earth
> and its works will be burned up. Since all these
> things are to be destroyed in this way, what sort of
> people ought you to be in holy conduct and godli-
> ness, looking for and hastening the coming of the
> day of God, because of which the heavens will be
> destroyed by burning, and the elements will melt
> with intense heat! But according to His promise
> we are looking for new heavens and a new earth, in
> which righteousness dwells. (2 Pet. 3:3–13)

One might ask, How can this be? This earth is a very stable place.
Let's think about this for a while. We have seen that God created the
universe, with the earth and the heavens with His power. So where is
that power or energy today? It is locked up in every material particle in
the universe, as well as in the things of the earth. And what is holding
the material earth together? Scripture tells us.

> He is the image of the invisible God, the firstborn
> of all creation. For by Him all things were created,
> both in the heavens and on earth, visible and invis-
> ible, whether thrones or dominions or rulers or
> authorities—all things have been created through
> Him and for Him. He is before all things, and in
> Him all things hold together. (Col. 1:15–17)

The Lord Jesus, who created all things, is also the one who holds
all things together. All He has to do is take His hands off the controls,
and what Peter describes will happen; this old earth will be gone. But
no worries! God has promised a new earth and heaven for those who
trust His Son.

> Then I saw a new heaven and a new earth; for the
> first heaven and the first earth passed away, and
> there is no longer any sea. (Rev. 21:1)

> "For behold, I create new heavens and a new earth;
> and the former things will not be remembered or
> come to mind. (Isa. 65:17)

> But according to His promise we are looking for
> new heavens and a new earth, in which righteous-
> ness dwells. (2 Pet. 3:13)

God's promise is not new, but it has been announced for ages by prophets and apostles. Three-fourth of the present earth is covered with water, but we are told the new earth will have no sea. This may concern those who love the ocean's coast. The raging ocean storms will no longer exist. Our present environment depends on the great ocean. The new earth will have a different, lasting environment for us to enjoy not requiring the sea; however, the new earth will have plenty of water for our enjoyment.

> I will give to the one who thirsts from the spring of
> the water of life without cost. (Rev. 21:6b)

> Then he showed me a river of the water of life, clear
> as crystal, coming from the throne of God and of
> the Lamb. (Rev. 22:1)

There will be water, but it will be more like the babbling brook that brings peace to the soul. Included with the New Earth will be the dwelling place the Lord Jesus promised to all those who are His.

> "And I saw the holy city, New Jerusalem, coming
> down out of heaven from God, made ready as a
> bride adorned for her husband." (Rev. 21:2)

The New Jerusalem comes down from heaven to the earth. It has been prepared in heaven, confirming Jesus' promise before he ascended that He was going to prepare a place for us. In Israel's culture, at the time, for a wedding, the groom came for his bride and ultimately took her to the home he had for her. So it is with the Lord Jesus; He will come for His bride, the Church, and take her to the new home He has prepared for her. This place, the New Jerusalem, is perfectly fit for the

Lord's bride, completely matching her character —so much so that the New Jerusalem is said to have been "made ready as a bride." The New Jerusalem will be a wonderful place. This city was looked forward to by Abraham.

> By faith he (Abraham) lived as an alien in the land of promise, as in a foreign land, dwelling in tents with Isaac and Jacob, fellow heirs of the same promise; for he was looking for the city, which has foundations, whose architect and builder is God. (Heb. 11:9–10)

Another Old Testament saint looking forward to the rewards of this city was Moses. He considered the lasting eternal rewards of this city as far greater riches than the treasures of Egypt, and Egypt was most likely the most advanced culture of Moses' day.

> By faith Moses, when he was born, was hidden for three months by his parents, because they saw he was a beautiful child; and they were not afraid of the king's edict. By faith Moses, when he had grown up, refused to be called the son of Pharaoh's daughter, choosing rather to endure ill treatment with the people of God than to enjoy the passing pleasures of sin, considering the reproach of Christ greater riches than the treasures of Egypt; for he was looking to the reward. (Heb. 11: 21–26)

God has long desired to dwell among His people. He walked in the garden with Adam and Eve. He dwelt in the midst of His people Israel as symbolized by the Shekinah Glory from the Tabernacle. Today He lives within His people, indwelling them by the Holy Spirit. In the new earth, God will dwell with His people forever.

> Moreover, I will make My dwelling among you, and My soul will not reject you. I will also walk among you and be your God, and you shall be My people. I am the Lord your God, who brought you

out of the land of Egypt so that you would not be their slaves, and I broke the bars of your yoke and made you walk erect. (Lev. 26:11–13)

And I heard a loud voice from the throne, saying, "Behold, the tabernacle of God is among men, and He will dwell among them, and they shall be His people, and God Himself will be among them, and He will wipe away every tear from their eyes; and there will no longer be any death; there will no longer be any mourning, or crying, or pain; the first things have passed away." (Rev. 21:3–4)

God will rule among His people, and they will gladly and willingly serve Him. They will be marked out as His and see Him face to face in a perfect relationship.

There will no longer be any curse; and the throne of God and of the Lamb will be in it/the city, and His bond-servants will serve Him; they will see His face, and His name will be on their foreheads. (Rev. 22:3–4)

Throughout the ages the tabernacle and temple represented the place where the Lord God dwelt in the midst of His people. In the New Jerusalem there will be no need for a temple to represent God's presence, for God and the Lamb will be there, and His people will be able to worship God and Son face to face. "I saw no temple in it, for the Lord God the Almighty and the Lamb are its temple." (Rev. 21:22)

At this time, heaven and earth will be merged. The New Jerusalem will be established on the earth, the home of God's forever family. God's purposes to have a family with whom He can relate and love will have been accomplished, and God will dwell among His people forever.

We can be certain God has a heavenly place ready for us; however, we do not know very much about what He has for us. There is a reason for this. What God has for us is so wonderful that it is impossible to put a description of it in the vernacular of us mortals so that we could understand. God has revealed a few details of heaven that we will look at.

First, we need to understand that what God begins, He will finish.

> "For I [Paul] am confident of this very thing, that
> He who began a good work in you will perfect it
> until the day of Christ Jesus." (Phil. 1:6)

God began a good work in the Garden of Eden, but sin and disobedience brought a curse and the resulting imperfections. Eden was a very physical place. God will restore a perfect physical creation in the New Earth. God will have His perfect creation.

Today many consider that heaven will be basically spiritual rather than physical. (You know, the thought of floating around on a cloud and playing a harp.) Sadly this is the result of Platonic philosophy creeping into our theology. Plato taught us that the material was bad or evil, and he stressed the spiritual with the result that much of our thinking today is untrue. God did not see anything wrong with the material. In fact, He saw His physical creation as being very good.

> "God saw all that He had made, and behold, it was
> very good (Gen. 1:31).

We are given a glimpse of the New Jerusalem as the Apostle John's vision is shared with us.

> Then one of the seven angels…came and spoke
> with me/John, saying, "Come here, I will show you
> the bride, the wife of the Lamb." And he carried me
> away in the Spirit to a great and high mountain,
> and showed me the holy city, Jerusalem, coming
> down out of heaven from God, having the glory of
> God. Her brilliance was like a very costly stone, as
> a stone of crystal-clear jasper. (Rev. 21:9–11)

John was unable to describe the radiance and brilliance of the city, except to use the things that were of value in his day—gems and precious stones. Around the city will be memorials to those who served God during this life. Examples are the tribes of Israel and the Apostles.

> It had a great and high wall, with twelve gates, and at the gates twelve angels; and names were written on them, which are the names of the twelve tribes and three gates on the south and three gates on the west. And the wall of the city had twelve foundation stones, and on them were the twelve names of the twelve apostles of the Lamb. (Rev. 21:12–14)

The size of the New Jerusalem is given. This size is huge, so much so that many doubt if the size can be taken literally. John refutes any claim that the description of the size is inaccurate by saying, "according to human measurements, which are also angelic measurements" (Rev. 21:17b).

> The one who spoke with me had a gold measuring rod to measure the city and its gates and its wall. The city is laid out as a square, and its length is as great as the width; and he measured the city with the rod, fifteen hundred miles; its length and width and height are equal. (Rev. 21:15–16)

Fifteen hundred square miles, this city will cover an area nearly the size of the western part of the United States. Yes, it is big; but it will be the home of the saints of all ages, and the Lord Jesus said He was going to prepare a place for us so we could all be together. But think about this: the height is equal to width and length, and the New Jerusalem comes down to the earth. Could this create a structural problem? During my career as a licensed Civil and Structural Engineer, I was faced with problems of how to support a structure. Many architectural designs looked great on paper, but finding ways to support the real structure and to keep it from collapsing in real life often takes some hours of pondering. I must admit that any problem I had was minor compared to this one, which makes me pleased that God is the engineer on this job. Some have suggested that the New Jerusalem will not be set on the New Earth; but it will orbit the New Earth like our present moon, in which case, there would be a rapid transit system between the New Jerusalem and the New Earth. There will be many things we will learn when God calls us home.

As an engineer, I have another issue that perplexes me.

> And the street of the city was pure gold, like transparent glass. (Rev. 21:21b)

As a Pavements Engineer, I worked with asphalt and concrete. Gold, though very precious, is not too durable or wear-resistant; however, it is possible that the streets of the New Jerusalem are only to compliment the brilliance of the city and not meant for vehicular traffic. Also, the answer may be that nothing wears out in heaven. Concerning vehicles, it's very likely that there won't be any in heaven when we get our resurrection bodies. (Won't our travel be like that of the Lord Jesus when he ascended from the Mount of Olives?)

Another significant quality of the New Earth is that it will be lighted by the glory of God. There will be no need for light from the sun or moon.

> And the city has no need of the sun or of the moon to shine on it, for the Glory of God has illumined it, and its lamp is the Lamb. The nations will walk by its light, and the kings of the earth will bring their glory into it. In the daytime (for there will be no night there) its gates will never be closed; and they will bring the glory and the honor of the nations into it; and nothing unclean, and no one who practices abomination and lying, shall ever come into it, but only those whose names are written in the Lamb's book of life. (Rev. 21:23–27)

> Your gates will be open continually; They will not be closed day or night, So that men may bring to you the wealth of the nations, With their kings led in procession.... No longer will you have the sun

for light by day, nor for brightness will the moon give you light; but you will have the Lord for an everlasting light. And your God for your glory. Your sun will no longer set, nor will your moon wane; for you will have the Lord for an everlasting light, and the days of your mourning will be over. (Isa. 60:11, 19–20)

Scripture only gives us a glimpse of conditions on the New Earth; however, the abundance of provisions for the saints is beyond question.

Then he showed me a river of the water of life, clear as crystal, coming from the throne of God and of the Lamb, in the middle of its street. On either side of the river was the tree of life, bearing twelve kinds of fruit, yielding its fruit every month; and the leaves of the tree were for the healing/nutrition of the nations. There will no longer be any curse. (Rev. 22:1–3a)

By the river on its bank, on one side and on the other, will grow all kinds of trees for food. Their leaves will not wither and their fruit will not fail. They will bear every month because their water flows from the sanctuary, and their fruit will be for food and their leaves for healing/nutrition." (Ezek. 47:12)

There is a river whose streams make glad the city of God, The holy dwelling places of the Most High. (Ps. 46:4)

We have seen earlier that God the Father, has promised all believers from the nations to the Son, if He would come to earth and provide redemption for men and women. Through the years, many rulers have tried asserting themselves into the position reserved only for Christ as King. God the Father only scoffs at them and warns them for the need to give homage to the Son. Psalm 2:1–12 gives us a beautiful picture of God the Father's thoughts.

> Why are the nations in an uproar And the peoples devising a vain thing? The kings of the earth take their stand and the rulers take counsel together against the Lord and against His Anointed, saying, "Let us tear their fetters apart and cast away their cords from us!" He who sits in the heavens laughs. The Lord scoffs at them. Then He will speak to them in His anger and terrify them in His fury, saying, "But as for Me, I have installed My King Upon Zion, My holy mountain." "I will surely tell of the decree of the Lord: He said to Me, 'You are My Son, Today I have begotten You. 'Ask of Me, and I will surely give the nations as Your inheritance, and the very ends of the earth as Your possession. 'You shall break them with a rod of iron, You shall shatter them like earthenware.'" Now therefore, O kings, show discernment; Take warning, O judges of the earth. Worship the Lord with reverence and rejoice with trembling. Do homage to the Son, that He not become angry, and you perish in the way; For His wrath may soon be kindled. How blessed are all who take refuge in Him!

The time foretold above will, at this time, be fulfilled. Jesus will reign forever as His Father has promised. Jesus will accomplish God's purpose for man to reign, but He will share this reign with those who the Father has given Him. They will also be fellow heirs with Jesus and be called His brothers.

> "If children, heirs also, heirs of God and fellow heirs with Christ, if indeed we suffer with Him so that we may also be glorified with Him." (Rom. 8:17)

> "For both He/Jesus who sanctifies and those who are sanctified are all from one Father; for which reason He is not ashamed to call them brethren" (Heb. 2:11)

> "And they will reign forever and ever." (Rev. 22:5b)

> But the Saints of the Highest One will receive the kingdom and possess the kingdom forever, for all ages to come.... Then the sovereignty, the dominion and the greatness of all the kingdoms under the whole heaven will be given to the people of the Saints of the Highest One; His kingdom will be an everlasting kingdom, and all the dominions will serve and obey Him. (Dan. 7:18, 27)

As we come to a conclusion we need to consider the final exhortations in the Book of Revelation. These are exhortations for the Lord to come, and His own call that He is coming. We need to be ready.

> Behold, I am coming quickly, and My reward is with Me, to render to every man according to what he has done. I am the Alpha and the Omega, the first and the last, the beginning and the end." Blessed are those who wash their robes, so that they may have the right to the tree of life, and may enter by the gates into the city.... The Spirit and the bride say, "Come." And let the one who hears say, "Come." And let the one who is thirsty come; let the one who wishes take the water of life without cost.... He who testifies to these things says, "Yes, I am coming quickly." Amen. Come, Lord Jesus. The grace of the Lord Jesus be with all. Amen. (Rev. 22:12–14, 17, 20–21)

We will pay particular attention to the Lord's own words. He says, "He is coming quickly." However, it has been over 1900 years since He returned to heaven. What the Lord is saying is not that He was coming soon necessarily but that His coming was imminent. He could come at any time, and men and women needed to be ready. Today, as we look at conditions in the world, His coming might not only be imminent; but it also may be soon.

It seems that to be with the Lord would be all we could desire; but secondly, the Lord says, "My reward is with me." Not only will we be with the Lord, but he also has rewards for those who are His. The Lord does appreciate those who serve Him, and He will show it when He comes. He leaves us on the earth for a purpose; we can still be earning rewards. They say, "You can't take it with you." However, you can send it on ahead!

> Do not store up for yourselves treasures on earth, where moth and rust destroy, and where thieves break in and steal. But store up for yourselves treasures in heaven, where neither moth nor rust destroys, and where thieves do not break in or steal. (Matt. 6:19–20)

Finally, we hear the bride saying come. This can be taken two ways: the bride saying, "Come Lord Jesus," or the bride calling to others to come to the Lord Jesus. We, the church, are the Lord's Bride. Are you anxious for the Lord to come? Are you asking others to come to Him?

The songwriters had it right.

> Oft-times the days seem long, our trials hard to
> bear,
> we're tempted to complain, to murmur and despair;
> but Christ will soon appear to catch His Bride
> away,
> all tears forever over in God's eternal day.
>
> It will be worth it all when we see Jesus,
> Life's trials seem so small when we see Christ;
> one glimpse of His dear face all sorrow will erase.
> So bravely run the race 'til we see Christ.

Thine is the glory, risen conquering Son,
Endless is the victory thou o'er death hast won.
Make us more than conquers, through Thy death-
      less love:
Bring us safe through Jordan to Thy home above.

Thine is the glory, Risen conquering Son;
Endless is the victory thou o'er death hast won.

HALLELUJAH! WHAT A SAVIOR!

ABOUT THE AUTHOR

Ron Sanders is a farm boy from Nebraska, who through the inspiration of an uncle decided to study engineering in college. Feeling a need for a broader understanding of life, he enrolled in seminary, and has combined the fields of engineering and the Bible as a means of livelihood and service to others. He and his wife have served Bible Study Fellowship International in the U.S., Canada and Asia, while he pursued an engineering career for the US Air Force. The couple has three grown children , seven grandchildren, and two great grandchildren.

They presently reside in Yakima Washington.

CPSIA information can be obtained
at www.ICGtesting.com
Printed in the USA
FSOW01n0140010515
6836FS

9 781634 177450